START TO FINISH

YACHTING

••••••••••••••••••••••

BARRY PICKTHALL

START TO FINISH

YACHTING

······························

BARRY PICKTHALL

WILEY ⊗ NAUTICAL

This edition first published 2009

© 2009 John Wiley and Sons, Ltd.

Registered office

John Wiley & Sons Ltd, The Atrium, Southern Gate, Chichester, West Sussex, PO19 8SQ, United Kingdom

For details of our global editorial offices, for customer services and for information about how to apply for permission to reuse the copyright material in this book please see our website at www.wiley.com.

We would like to thank A&C Black for their kind permission to reproduce material from Andy du Port and Neville Featherstone's Reeds Almanac 2009, Adlard Coles Nautical, an imprint of A&C Black Publishers

Library of Congress Cataloging-in-Publication Data

Pickthall, Barry
Yachting: start to finish / Barry Pickthall
p. cm.
Includes index.

ISBN 978-0-470-69752-8 (pbk. : alk. paper) 1. Yachting--Handbooks, manuals, etc. I. Title
GV813.P53 2009
797.124'6--dc22

2009015938

ISBN 978-0-470-69752-8

Designed and typeset in 8.5pt Frutiger LT Std by PPL Ltd
Illustrations by Greg Filip/PPL

Printed and bound by SNP Leefung Printers Ltd, China

Contents

Getting started

My introduction to sailing began when I was a child, learning the ropes in a family dinghy. It was not until my teenage years that the opportunity came to sail offshore. It began with a blast aboard an Iroquois fast cruising catamaran. The winds were blowing force 4-5 and I dearly wanted all sail up and to lift a hull as we broad reached across the waves. Our skipper was far more circumspect. He put two reefs in the mainsail before we had even left our sheltered mooring, and called for the smallest jib once we were outside the harbour.

We still managed to exceed 10 knots, but I well remember the frustration felt at the time. He was right of course. In a dinghy, you are taught to extract the maximum from the boat, for the worst that can happen is to capsize and get wet. With much heavier keelboats and cruising yachts, the loads are exponentially higher.

Loadings apart, the differences between sailing a dinghy and a yacht are not so far apart. Certainly the basics are the same. One significant advantage keelboats have is that, thanks to their heavy keels, they don't capsize! The major disadvantage is that because of their greater draught, keelboats are all too easy to run aground and stay there – unless of course you have one of the Southerly yachts featured in this book with a swing keel that can be raised and lowered at the press of a button!

Nowadays, many people discover the delights of sailing later in life, bypass the traditional dinghy inauguration altogether and are introduced through friends or experiences on holiday, straight to cruising yachts and keelboats.

That's fine, but buying a yacht is often one of the biggest expenditures many of us will make, so it is prudent to know what you are doing before going afloat, or at least to have an experienced hand onboard to show you the ropes. Better still, enrol on an introductory sailing course like those organized by the UKSA to learn not just the rudiments of getting a boat to go where you want it to, but how to dock, reef, communicate and navigate safely. These are all essential skills, and your choice of boat will be all the more informed once you are competent – and confident – enough, to sail her away for a weekend.

This keelboat/cruising manual takes you through a step-by-step guide based on the UKSA's teaching programs and is designed to provide readers with a thorough grounding to enable you to sail a yacht safely.

Sailing is a great participation sport, accessible to all ages. Disability is no handicap either. With audible compasses to guide the blind, sliding seats for paraplegics and wheelchair access or hoists now available on even modest yachts, everyone has the opportunity to get afloat.
You will love it!

Barry Pickthall

Parts of the boat

- **Jib**
Foresail.

- **Foredeck/bow buoyancy tank**
Buoyancy to keep the bow up when boat is flooded.

- **Mast**

- **Mainsail**
Sail attached to mast and boom.

- **Shrouds**
Side stays holding up the mast.

- **Starboard side**
Right hand side of the boat.

- **Side deck**
Shaped to sit on and balance the boat against the heeling force of the wind.

- **Port side**
Left hand side of the boat.

- **Sit-in bars**
Safety grab rail to stop crew from hiking outboard.

- **Boom**

- **Cockpit**
Crew area within the boat.

- **Mainsheet**
System to control mainsail angle and tension.

- **Gunwale**
Outside edge of the boat.

- **Tiller**
Used to control rudder

- **Retractable bowsprit**
To set the asymmetric spinnaker from.

- **Transom scuppers**
Holes in transom to allow water to escape the cockpit after flooding.

- **Bow**
The stem or front end of the boat

- **Boom vang (Gnav)**
To control sail shape and leech tension.

- **Gooseneck**
Hinged connection linking boom to mast.

- **Jib fairlead**
Adjustable lead for sheet rope that controls the jib or headsail.

- **Stern/transom**
Aft end of the boat.

- **Tiller extension**
Attached to the tiller by a universal joint, this extends the reach of the tiller to allow the helmsman to control the rudder when sitting out.

- **Bulb keel (lifts for towing)**
High aspect weighted foil to counter sideways and heeling forces of the sails.

- **Fixed rudder**
Controls the direction of the boat.

- **Hull**
Outer shell of the boat.

- VHF aerial and wind vane
- Electronic masthead instruments
- Masthead
- Cap shrouds
- Backstay
- Sail battens
- Boom topping lift
- Mainsail reefing points
- Mainsail
- Companionway hatch
- Headsail winch
- Boom
- Lifelines
- Twin steering wheels
- Pushpit
- Twin rudders

- Electronic radar transmitter aerial
- Headsail furling top swivel
- Spreaders (crosstrees)
- Furling headsail
- Mast
- Lower shrouds
- Headsail sheets
- Headsail furling drum
- Pulpit
- Foredeck
- Boom vang
- Genoa track
- Mainsheet
- Mainsheet traveller
- Halyard/reefing winch
- Keel

The science of sailing

The sight of a jumbo jet coming slowly into land with wings and wheels extended always leaves me in awe. How can something weighing 380 tonnes fly so slowly without falling out of the sky? The answer is the same as that to the common question about sailing: How can a yacht sail as close as 40° to the wind?

It is all about aerodynamics and the pressure differentials on one side of a wing, compared to the other. The aeroplane wing has more curvature on its upper surface. As it moves forward, the airflow streaming across has to travel faster over a longer distance to meet up with the air flowing along the flatter lower surface. This difference in speed leads to a drop in pressure on the upper surface, which results in lift. The faster the plane's speed the greater this becomes, to the point where the differential in pressure between the upper and lower sections of the wing is sufficient to raise the weight of the plane off the ground.

The same happens over the surface of a sail. The airflow across the back or leeward side travels faster than the air flowing across the windward side. The resulting pressure differentials create the lift that drives the yacht forward.

This force within the sail would drive the sailboat sideways were it not for the lateral resistance of the yacht's keel. The best demonstration of this is to hold a knife blade in water and move it about, first up and down, and then sideways, when you will feel the lateral resistance. It is the balance in design between the sails and shape of the

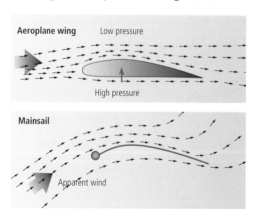

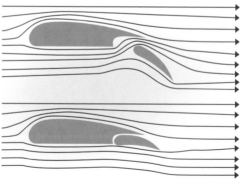

Aeroplane wing with adjustable slat used to increase lift at low speeds

hull that determines the efficiency with which a boat sails to windward.

Load - carrying sailing ships from the past were shaped like pointed bricks and only gained a spring in their step when the wind was abeam or behind. If it was nearer to the bow, they had no chance of making any headway. Indeed, vessels caught by head winds for any length of time when going west-about around Cape Horn, would eventually turn and sail around the world the other way rather than waste time attempting to buck into it.

By contrast, a modern keelboat like the Laser SB3 sails very efficiently to windward, providing the crew position their weight to balance out the heeling force of the wind. This efficiency is enhanced by the jib or forward sail, which induces a slot effect in the same way that extending slats on a plane wing improves lift coefficient at slow speeds when taking off and landing. Airflow narrows and accelerates through the 'slot' between jib and mainsail, improving the lift coefficient.

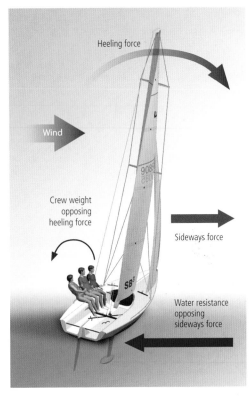

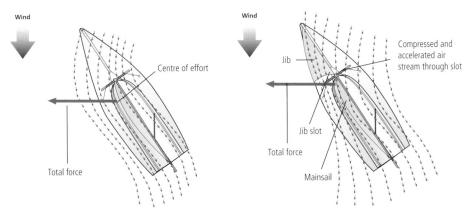

The jib channels the air through the slot between the fore and aft sails, speeding the flow around the back of the mainsail to further improve the pressure differential between the windward and leeward sides.

Centre of effort

Modern keelboats are so well-balanced that it is quite possible to alter course by adjusting the sails alone. Indeed, instructors at the UKSA will show students how they can vary the centre of effort within the sail plan and the direct effect this has on the course that the yacht sails. They learn that by letting out the jib (which has the effect of moving the centre of effort aft) the yacht will point closer to the wind. Conversely, releasing the mainsail and sheeting in the jib moves the centre of effort forward and change the balance of the boat, giving it a tendency to bear away from the wind.

Apparent wind

Apparent wind is the actual flow of air acting on the sail as the boat moves forward and differs in speed and direction from the true or prevailing wind experienced by a stationary observer.

When sailing, the apparent wind is the important factor when determining the sheeting angle for sails. The faster the yacht travels, the further the apparent wind angle moves forward and the greater its velocity. Wind indicators on the yacht measure apparent wind. Stationary indicators such as flags on land or moored vessels show the true wind.

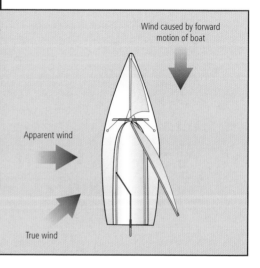

The centre of effort is a point within the sail plan where, if it was a card cut-out, it could be balanced on the tip of a pin. This centre point within the rig must be in balance with the centre of resistance of the underwater portion of the hull, a point on the keel. The closer these two points are in the vertical plane the finer the balance will be. This is important to remember when reefing in stronger winds. If you simply take in area on the mainsail and do not change the jib area accordingly, the yacht will exhibit lee helm and will want to bear off from the wind all the time. Conversely, if you take down the jib and do not reduce the size of the mainsail, the yacht will naturally keep pointing up into wind and be very heavy on the helm, known as weather helm.

Driving force of the wind

Close-hauled sailing to windward. The strong lateral force of the wind on the sails is countered by the lateral resistance of the keel, which leads to forward drive up to 40° off the wind.

Reaching beam onto the wind. The most efficient angle of sail. With the sails let out, or sheets eased, as sailors like to call it, the lateral force of the wind is reduced and the energy produced by the sails provides additional driving force.

Running before the wind. With no airflow across the sails, and no apparent wind benefit, all the wind energy goes into pushing the boat forward. Because of the 90° angle of the sails to the wind, the flow between the two sides of the aerofoil is reduced dramatically. As a result, the boat will never sail faster than the speed of the wind.

Points of sail

When sailing, the strength and direction of the wind are all-important. Look around you and see which way flags are flying. You can also feel the wind and sense its direction by turning your face. Your ears are highly tuned to sensing wind, as well as sound. When you change from one point of sail to another, the sails, and crew positions must also be adjusted to match the yacht's balance and heading towards or away from the wind.

■ Close-hauled: Sailing about 45° from the wind

This is beating to windward with sails sheeted in hard, and crew weight on an open keelboat, like the Laser SB3, out on the windward side to balance the boat.

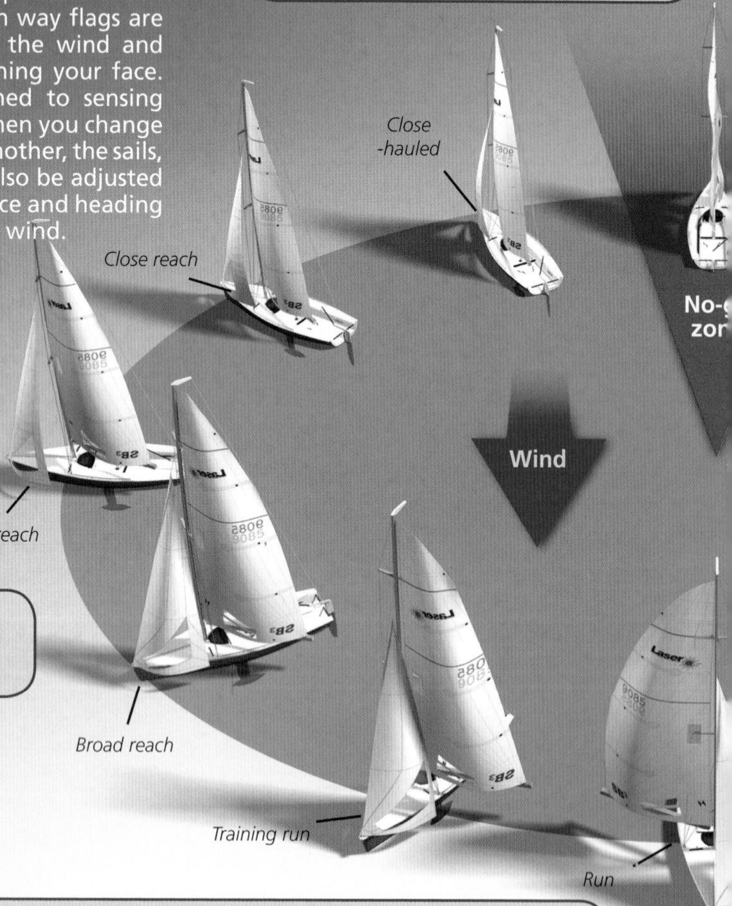

Close-hauled

Close reach

No-
zor

Beam reach

Wind

■ Broad reach: 120-160° from the wind

Broad reach

Training run

Run

■ Run: 175-180° from the wind

Sailing directly downwind either on port or starboard gybe. Sails are eased right out, the jib can be set on the opposite side to the mainsail (goose-winged) to project greater area to the wind.

■ Head to wind

This is the no-go zone and extends about 45° either side of the oncoming wind direction. Turn too high into the wind and the sails will start to flap, the boat will slow and eventually drift backwards. The only way to make progress is to sail at about 45° either side of the wind with sails sheeted in hard, and make a zigzag course. This is called beating to windward.

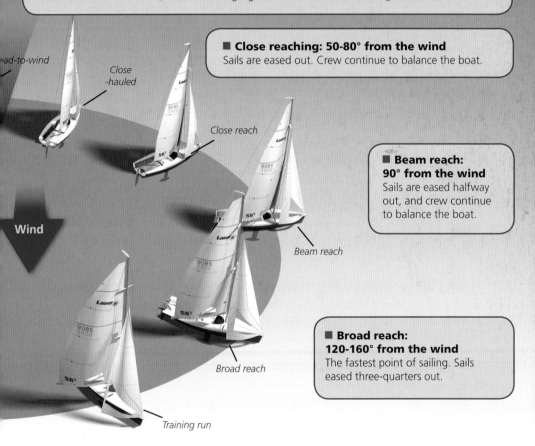

ad-to-wind

Close
-hauled

Close reach

■ Close reaching: 50-80° from the wind

Sails are eased out. Crew continue to balance the boat.

■ Beam reach:
90° from the wind

Sails are eased halfway out, and crew continue to balance the boat.

Beam reach

Wind

Broad reach

■ Broad reach:
120-160° from the wind

The fastest point of sailing. Sails eased three-quarters out.

Training run

■ Training run: 170° from the wind

The safest angle for novices to sail downwind.

Choosing a yacht

Racing, the saying goes, improves the breed. That is certainly the case with yacht design which, in five decades, has progressed from traditional narrow, heavy displacement hulls with integral keel and rudder to much more efficient wide beam, light displacement forms with all manner of keel and rudder configurations. Their greater hull volume, developed to increase form stability and improve performance off wind, has the practical benefit for cruising designs of packing more berths, a fully fitted galley and bathroom (we still call them heads) into even the most modest sized yachts.

Racing has led to a marked change in profile shapes too. The graceful raked bows have given way to vertical stem shapes drawn to extend the waterline length and minimise weight in the ends and the sickening pitching moment that yachts with long overhangs develop when riding through waves. There is a financial advantage too, for by minimising length in this way, berthing fees are proportionally less as well. The reverse transom, another weight saving solution drawn from the racing world, is now firmly embraced by cruising yacht builders to provide a swim platform and easy boarding route from the dinghy. The most popular underwater configuration is the fin

Southerly 46 RST yacht.

keel and spade rudder similar to that on the Laser SB3. Being a trailable sports keelboat, this fin retracts like a dagger board so that it can be launched and recovered in shallow water from its road trailer, rather than have to be lifted in and out by crane.

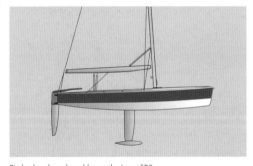
Fin keel and spade rudder on the Laser SB3.

Some multihulls employ the same concept with a lifting dagger board fitted in each hull, though unlike a keelboat, they have positive buoyancy and are not weighted, which makes them easy to lift up and down.

The concept of retractable keels has been taken to a high level by Northshore Yachts, builders of the Southerly range of swing keel cruising yachts, to provide the freedom to navigate shallow channels and beach the boat,

Lagoon 380 cruising catamaran.

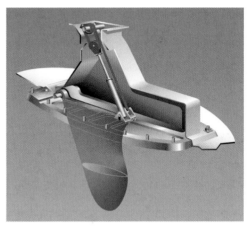

Swing keel configuration on the Southerly range of yachts.

coupled with the performance and greater stability offered by deep draught keels. The cast-iron, aerofoil-shaped keel pivots within a grounding plate and is raised and lowered

Cruising multihulls, generally catamarans, have other advantages over monohulls, including greater speed off wind, a large foredeck for sunbathing and enormous volume below decks consisting of a wide communal cabin across the bridge deck and private sleeping quarters split between the two hulls. Their greatest attribute in many eyes, however, is the fact that multihulls don't heel over like monohulls, but they are more susceptible to weight increases. A full complement of crew and their attendant gear invariably saps their speed advantage.

Southerly 43 RST swing keel yacht safely beached.

at the push of a button operating an hydraulic ram. The cast-iron grounding plate has several functions: it serves as fixed ballast, provides a strong pivot point for the keel, and protects the bottom of the boat when drying out. This lifting keel works in conjunction with twin spade rudders, set either side of the stern, which act like two legs of a tripod to maintain a level stance when taking to the ground.

The twin rudder configuration is another idea to spring from racing. This is a common concept within the wide Open 60 style ocean racing yachts, and being splayed out at 20° or more from vertical, the leeward foil continues to provide perfect control even when the hull is well heeled.

Bilge keels are another popular concept for shoal draught cruising yachts. The twin keels are not as efficient as a single foil when sailing to windward, but their simplicity provides an inexpensive option, especially for people who have a half tide mooring or wish to cruise in areas where harbours dry out.

Physics dictates that the lower the centre of gravity, the greater the stability. Designers have tackled this in several ways. One is the addition of a bulb or ballast wings attached to the bottom of the keel that not only improve the stability factor, but also provide an end-plate effect to the tip of the foil, improving hydrostatic flow.

Twin rudders can provide better control when the yacht is heeled.

A typical bilge keeled yacht.

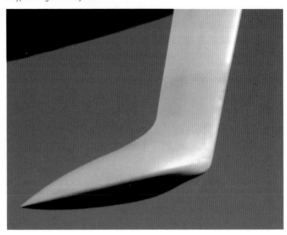
Bulb keel designed to maximize stability.

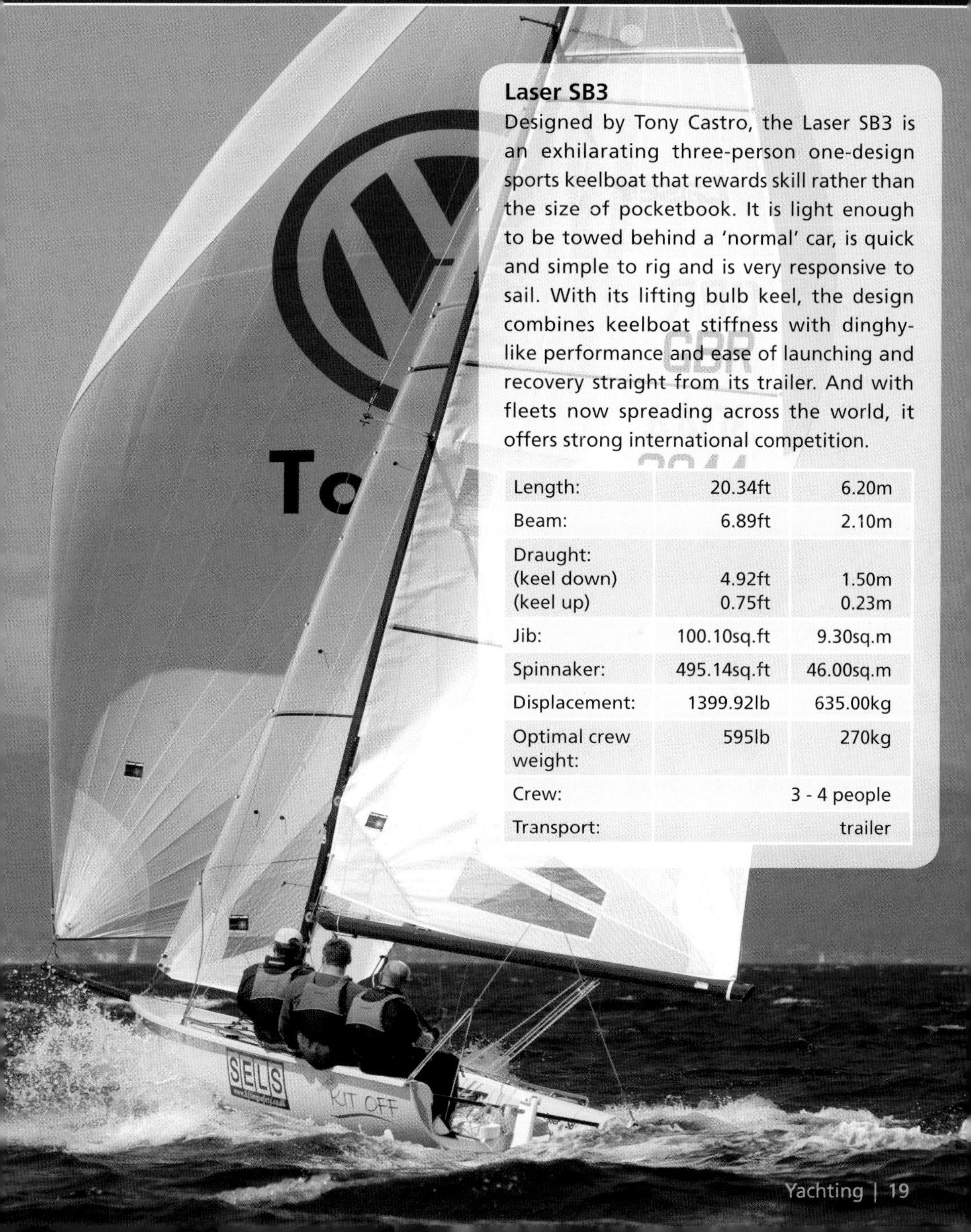

Laser SB3

Designed by Tony Castro, the Laser SB3 is an exhilarating three-person one-design sports keelboat that rewards skill rather than the size of pocketbook. It is light enough to be towed behind a 'normal' car, is quick and simple to rig and is very responsive to sail. With its lifting bulb keel, the design combines keelboat stiffness with dinghy-like performance and ease of launching and recovery straight from its trailer. And with fleets now spreading across the world, it offers strong international competition.

Length:	20.34ft	6.20m
Beam:	6.89ft	2.10m
Draught: (keel down) (keel up)	4.92ft 0.75ft	1.50m 0.23m
Jib:	100.10sq.ft	9.30sq.m
Spinnaker:	495.14sq.ft	46.00sq.m
Displacement:	1399.92lb	635.00kg
Optimal crew weight:	595lb	270kg
Crew:		3 - 4 people
Transport:		trailer

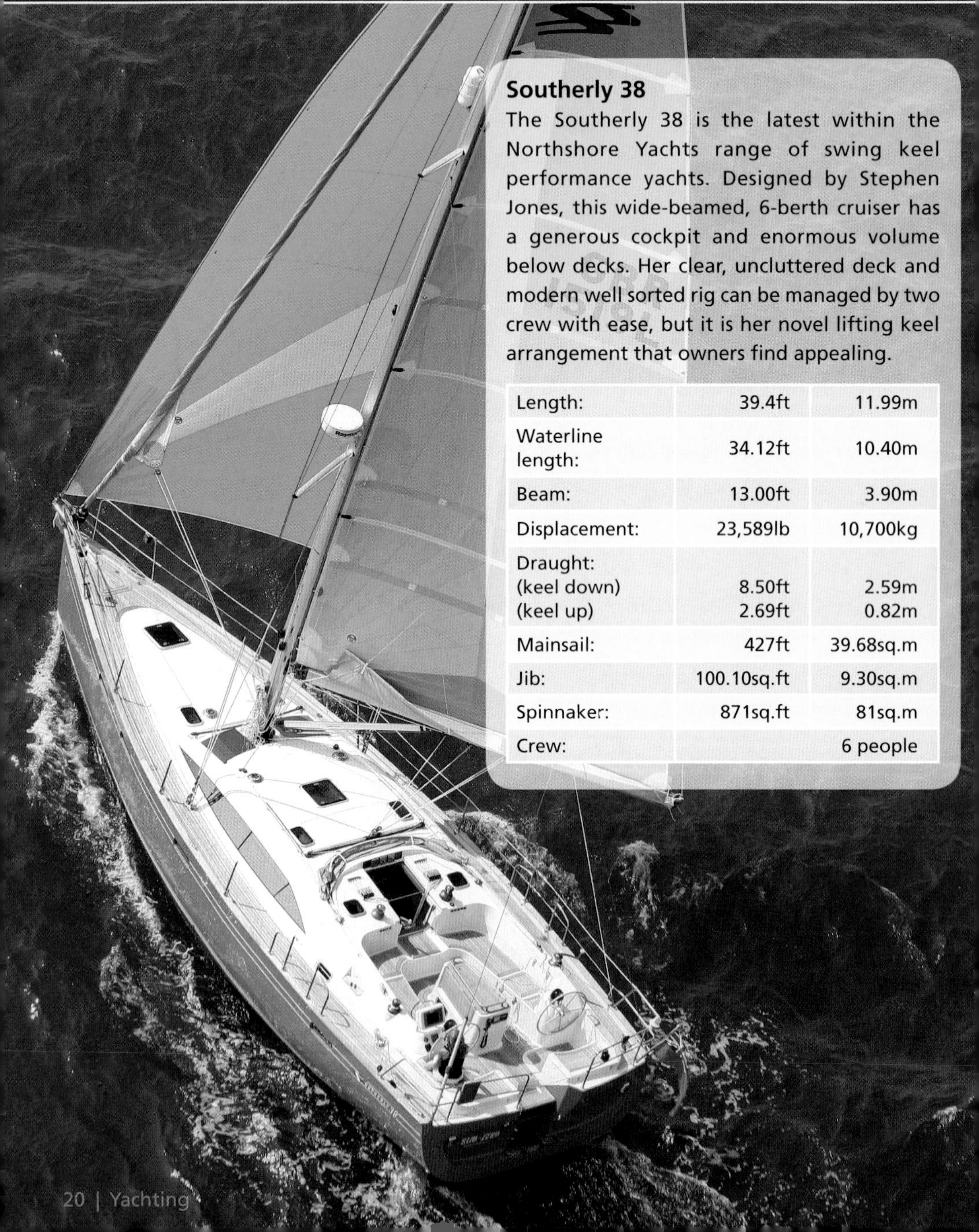

Southerly 38

The Southerly 38 is the latest within the Northshore Yachts range of swing keel performance yachts. Designed by Stephen Jones, this wide-beamed, 6-berth cruiser has a generous cockpit and enormous volume below decks. Her clear, uncluttered deck and modern well sorted rig can be managed by two crew with ease, but it is her novel lifting keel arrangement that owners find appealing.

Length:	39.4ft	11.99m
Waterline length:	34.12ft	10.40m
Beam:	13.00ft	3.90m
Displacement:	23,589lb	10,700kg
Draught: (keel down) (keel up)	8.50ft 2.69ft	2.59m 0.82m
Mainsail:	427ft	39.68sq.m
Jib:	100.10sq.ft	9.30sq.m
Spinnaker:	871sq.ft	81sq.m
Crew:		6 people

Types of rig

Bermudan masthead sloop
The traditional cruising rig with triangular mainsail and full height overlapping genoa.

Cutter rig
Similar to a Bermudan masthead rig, but with a staysail set as an intermediate sail between the genoa and mainsail.

Fractional rig
The modern alternative to the Bermudan rig. The smaller jib makes the sail easier to handle and extra area is carried in the mainsail to compensate.

Yawl rig
A two-masted rig with the mizzen set behind the rudder. The mizzen sail is smaller than on a ketch rig.

Ketch rig
A two-masted rig with the aft mizzen mast set ahead of the rudder. A popular rig for blue water voyaging because the individual sails are smaller and thus easier to handle.

Gaff rig
A traditional sail plan with a quadrilateral mainsail supported at the top by a gaff spar.

Cat/Freedom rig
A simple rig popular in the USA with a large mainsail set on an unstayed mast close to the bows. The modern Freedom version with a wishbone boom, similar to those used on sailboards, has found favour with some blue water cruising enthusiasts.

Buying a yacht

It could be one of the most expensive purchases you make, so deposits and payments should be protected just as if you were buying a property.

If you are buying through a dealer or from stock, ensure that the company operates a client account and make payments payable directly to that account.

Check that the contract contains a full specification or inventory. If stage payments are used to purchase hull mouldings, engines, sails, rigging and equipment, ensure that title for these items are transferred to you, clearly identified to the hull number, and insured.

If buying second-hand, check to see whether the yacht is subject to a mortgage. If it is, this will be listed on the boat's registration documents and recorded in the Small Ships Register.

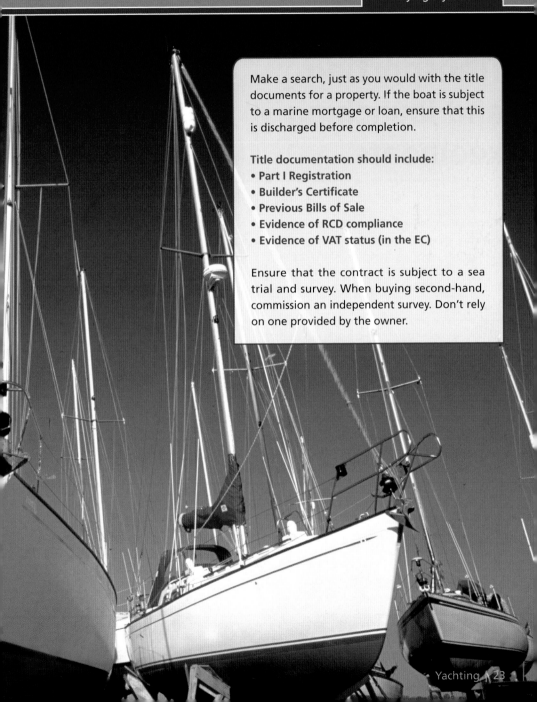

Make a search, just as you would with the title documents for a property. If the boat is subject to a marine mortgage or loan, ensure that this is discharged before completion.

Title documentation should include:
- **Part I Registration**
- **Builder's Certificate**
- **Previous Bills of Sale**
- **Evidence of RCD compliance**
- **Evidence of VAT status (in the EC)**

Ensure that the contract is subject to a sea trial and survey. When buying second-hand, commission an independent survey. Don't rely on one provided by the owner.

Transporting and launching keelboats

Sports keelboats like the Laser SB3 are designed to be dry sailed: stored ashore on their trailers during the week so that they don't attract weed or require antifouling, and launched and recovered on their trailer each time they are sailed. Many sailing clubs and marinas now have a secure pen to store the boats in and a slipway or crane to get them in and out of the water, but it is almost just as easy to drop the mast and tow the boat home.

Towing regulations in many countries stipulate that the dry weight of the towing vehicle must, at a minimum, equal the weight of the trailer, which should also have brakes. Some countries also restrict the driving age to those over 21 who must also pass an additional test, so do check that your driving licence allows you to tow a heavy trailer and your vehicle is compatible before setting out on the road.

The SB3 weighs 1,400lb (635kg) and with her keel up draws only 9in (23cm) of water so can be towed behind any mid-range family car. Larger boats like the J24 and J80, which have fixed keels, may require a larger vehicle to tow them and a dockside crane or hoist to lift them in and out of the water.

❶ Ensure the trailer is loaded slightly front heavy to avoid it 'snaking' out of control when braking.

❺ Sort out the shrouds and halyards before lifting the mast.

2 Loop the safety wire around the ball hitch and lock the jockey wheel in place.

3 Put the trailer jacks down before climbing onto the trailer.

4 The temporary crane used to lift and lower the SB3's keel in position.

6 Connect the foot of the mast to the step.

7 Connect the side shrouds to chain plates.

8 Hoist the mast using the trailer winch.

9 Connect forestay to stem fitting.

10 Secure shrouds with tape.

11 Connect jib hanks to forestay.

12 Use a rope between car and trailer when launching to extend the distance the trailer can go in the water.

15 Ease boat off trailer, keeping a firm hold of the painter.

16 Fit the rudder.

17 Turn boat head to wind and hoist the mainsail.

⑬ Communicate with the driver using hand signals.

⑭ Disconnect the boat from the trailer.

⑱ Set sail slides in mast track.

⑲ Connect the sail controls....

⑳ Hoist the jib...and you are ready to go sailing.

The rig

With one-design classes like the Laser SB3, mast, boom, rigging and sails are all uniform, but with many production cruising designs, the rig can vary from one boat to another.

The first check is to ensure that the mast is a tight fit in its step, and in the case of keel stepped masts, at the deck gate too. If there is any play at either point, the mast will pivot and bend uncontrollably when sailing, negating all the careful tuning you undertake.

When setting up the rigging for the first time, it is essential that the mast is vertical and rig tension equal on each side. A tension gauge offers the most accurate way to measure this and replicate the settings.

Masthead Rigs

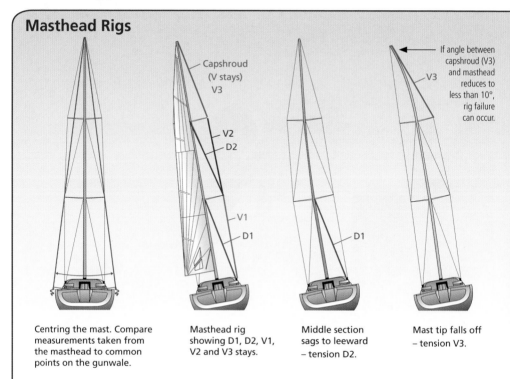

Capshroud
(V stays)
V3

V2
D2

V1
D1

D1

V3

If angle between capshroud (V3) and masthead reduces to less than 10°, rig failure can occur.

Centring the mast. Compare measurements taken from the masthead to common points on the gunwale.

Masthead rig showing D1, D2, V1, V2 and V3 stays.

Middle section sags to leeward – tension D2.

Mast tip falls off – tension V3.

The masthead rig is relatively simple to control and tune. The designer will have been able to calculate the position of the mast and the optimum amount of rake required quite accurately, leaving you with the relatively simple job of fine-tuning it to take account of changes in the centre of lateral resistance and effort caused by the heel and changes in sail trim (see page 12). These two points are only brought back into balance by the rudder.

If the rudder angle, or weight on the helm, is excessive the mast needs to be moved forward, or aft when there is little or no weight on the helm. The optimum angle of weather helm (a natural tendency to point up into wind) in force 2-3 winds is 3°. If it is less than this, then the yacht is likely to exhibit lee helm (a natural tendency to bear away). If the rudder angle is more than 5° above its neutral position, the mast should be moved forward one notch at a time to reduce this angle and weight on the helm. Once the rig has been stepped, fine tuning the mast can be undertaken in moderate winds of force 2-3. Start sailing to windward on one tack with full sail and check up the mast for any deflection and adjust accordingly. Then go about and repeat the process on the opposite tack.

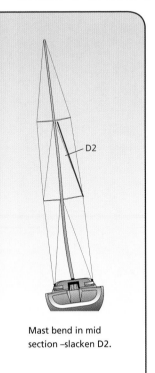

D2

Mast bend in mid section –slacken D2.

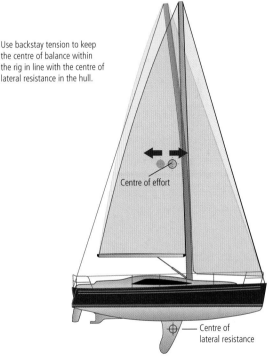

Use backstay tension to keep the centre of balance within the rig in line with the centre of lateral resistance in the hull.

Centre of effort

Centre of lateral resistance

Pointing ability

Mast rake also has a bearing on pointing ability. Sailmakers suggest an angle of between 0.5° and 1° as a rule of thumb for masthead rigs. If additional rake improves pointing ability but also increases weather helm, then push the mast step forward a notch and shorten the forestay to maintain the same degree of rake. Pre-bend, or permanent fore and aft set in the mast is not encouraged within a masthead rig, though adjustment of backstay tension, reducing it when sailing with the wind astern, and re-tensioning it when beating, will help to keep the centre of lateral resistance and effort in line, and lead to a speed advantage.

Lateral support

Unlike fractional configurations, masthead rigs must be kept in column even in heavy winds. If there is any tendency to bend sideways, this not only slackens the forestay, increasing curvature in headsail shape just when you want the flattest possible entry, but can lead to mast failure.

The most critical element is the angle between the masthead and cap shroud. If this falls below 10°, then the leverage on the shroud can become strong enough to break the wire or its supporting spreader.

Fractional rig

Unless the rig is fitted with swept-back spreaders to provide the triangular support for the rig, (pictured right) running check stays and the backstay play an essential role in controlling the fore and aft bend and stop the mast from 'pumping' in a seaway.

The upper runners, which require a purchase in the order of 44:1, control the headstay tension and thus the shape of the genoa. The lower runners control the shape of the mainsail and check the mast from bending too far forward. This has less tension and, like the backstay, can usually be controlled with a 5:1 purchase. The backstay provides support for the mast when gybing.

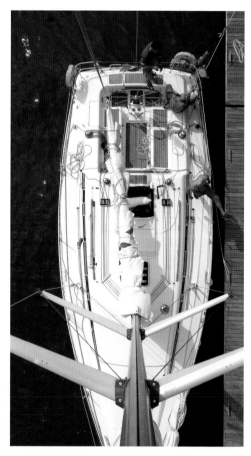

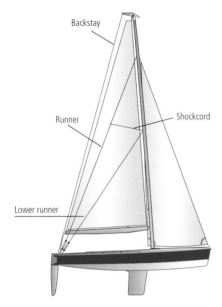

Backstay

Runner

Shockcord

Lower runner

Side bend

Unlike masthead configurations, some side bend at the top of the mast can improve sail balance. A fractionally rigged yacht with no tip bend will be more tender when going to windward than one with a well-tuned mast where the tip of the spar bends off to leeward in the gusts. This is because the tip acts as a shock absorber, opening the leech of the mainsail and depowering the rig automatically. The boat is thus stiffer and faster to windward.

Tuning a multi-spreader fractional rig is much more time-consuming than a masthead one and needs to be done in force 2-3 conditions with full main and headsail set. You can start at the dock by setting the forestay to

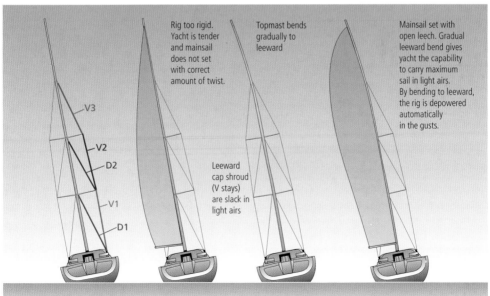

V3

V2
D2

V1

D1

Rig too rigid. Yacht is tender and mainsail does not set with correct amount of twist.

Topmast bends gradually to leeward

Leeward cap shroud (V stays) are slack in light airs

Mainsail set with open leech. Gradual leeward bend gives yacht the capability to carry maximum sail in light airs. By bending to leeward, the rig is depowered automatically in the gusts.

the required rake (3° is a good starting point) and checking that the mast is centred at deck level and the lower and intermediate shrouds are adjusted equally until hand tight.

The object is to set the lower shrouds up with greater tension than the D2s and for the cap or V shrouds to come under load only when the winds are above 5 knots apparent. The rig is then fine-tuned by sailing to windward under full sail and making small changes to the leeward turnbuckles (no more than one or two turns at a time) before tacking and checking the results, until you get a uniform bend on either tack. Never adjust the weather shrouds when they are under load.

Tip

Remember to lock off the turnbuckles and, for additional security, wire or split pin them together and tape over. Spreader tips should also be swathed in tape to protect the sails.

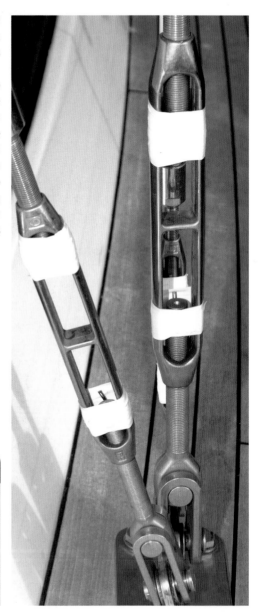

Knots, ropes and running rigging

The best way to learn knots is to carry a piece of thin cord in your pocket and practise during quiet moments until you can do them with your eyes shut.

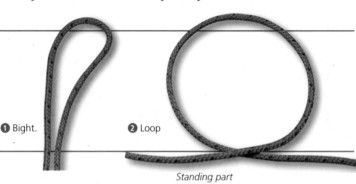

■ Bight and loop
The first nautical terms to learn.

❶ Bight.

❷ Loop

Standing part

■ Reef knot
Used to tie two lines of equal thickness together, such as reefing lines and sail ties. Remember the rule: Left over right. Right over left.

❶ Bring the two ends of the rope together, cross left over right and tuck under.

❷ Continuing with the same end, cross right over left and tuck under.

❸ Pull tight and check.

For an interactive lesson, go to **www.uksa.org/ knotmaster** and master 5 knots in 5 days.

■ Figure-of eight knot
Stopper knot tied into the ends of sheets and halyards to stop them from running out through a block or sheet fairlead.

❶ Form a loop.

❶ Form a crossing turn in the end of the rope.

❷ Form the loop (rabbit hole) to the size required, with the outer end upward.

■ Bowline

Ties a nonslip knot in the end of a rope. Used to form a secure loop in the end of a mooring line or to tie a sheet to the clew of a sail. Remember the adage: *The rabbit comes out of its hole runs round the tree then goes back down the hole again.*

❸ Round the back of the standing part.

❹ And guide it down through the small loop.

❺ Pull the end through the small loop.

❻ Pull tight and check the tail is long enough not to pull out.

❷ Pass the end round the back of the standing part.

❸ Return the end through the loop.

❹ Pull tight.

■ Admiralty stopper knot

A more permanent stopper knot tied into the ends of sheets and halyards on larger yachts that will not 'wash out' when dragged in the water or washed down the deck like the figure-of-eight knot.

❶ Form a bight.

❷ Wrap the working end around the bight four times.

❸ Pass the end through the loop.

❹ Pull the standing part tight to tighten the loop.

❶ Form a bight in the thicker rope.

❷ Pass the end of the thinner rope up through the bight and under.

❸ Pass the end of the thinner rope under its own standing part.

❹ Pull tight.

■ Single sheet bend

Used to tie two lines of unequal thickness together, such as sail ties.

■ Coiling rope

Loose rope ends like halyard tails should be coiled and secured with the tail so that they are ready to be shaken out at a moment's notice.

■ Cam cleat

Pull the rope down through the twin spring-loaded cams and allow the load on the rope to hold it tight. To clear, simply pull the rope tail upwards.

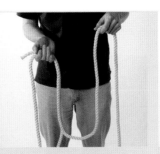

❶ Take the end of the rope in one hand, stretch it out with the other, twist it clockwise...

❷ ...and transfer each loop to the first hand.

❸ Once coiled, make several turns with the working end around the coils and feed through the top loop...

❹ ...and pull tight.

■ Clam cleat

This simple cleat has no moving parts. Steer the rope into the jaws and allow the load on the rope to draw it down into the grooves and lock it. Works best with three-stranded ropes. To clear, simply pull the rope tail upwards.

■ Cleating a rope

The OXO method of tying off a mooring line or halyard on a horn cleat.

❶ Take a full turn around the cleat.   ❷ Cross over in a figure-of-eight....   ❸ ...and finish with a final turn around the cleat.

■ Rope clutch

Often sited in groups and in line with a winch on either side of the companionway hatch, these stopper cleats, provide a neat solution to holding halyard, reefing and vang lines led back from mast to cockpit. To operate:

❶ Lift the clutch lever.
❷ Pull the slack through.
❸ Then wrap 3 turns around the winch and tension as required.

❹ Push the clutch lever back down to lock, then release line from the winch.

To release:

❶ Take 3 turns round the winch and take up the tension on the line before releasing the clutch.

❷ Check that there are no knots in the rope tail, release the clutch lever and free the line from the winch.

■ Stowing halyards

When halyard cleats are mast mounted and there is no bag to stow them in, hang the coil securely on the horn cleat.

❶ Make up the coil.
❷ Take the first coil leading back to the cleat and pass it through the centre.
❸ Twist this a couple of times to form a small diameter loop at the end over the top horn as a retaining line.

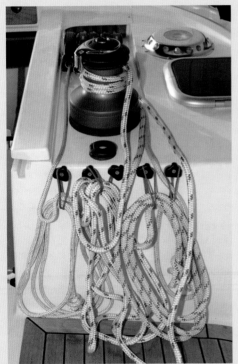

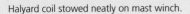
Control lines held in shock cord holders in the cockpit.

Halyard coil stowed neatly on mast winch.

What to wear

You are going to get wet, so be prepared… to enjoy it! Unless you are sailing in the tropics, wearing the right clothing to keep you warm and dry is the first requisite to maximising enjoyment afloat. There is a wide variety of specialist clothing available. The challenge in hot, humid, energy-sapping sailing environments is for climate - related clothing that will keep you dry inside and out.

The latest open keelboat orientated garments combine lightweight, breathable outer jacket and hi-fit trousers designed for fast and furious movement that weigh in a third the weight of offshore oilskins.

Another option, especially in colder regions, is a drysuit over coating warm underclothes or a drytop with rubber sealed collar and cuffs worn in conjunction with high-fit waterproof trousers. Unlike a wetsuit, the drysuit and drytop are designed to keep the body dry. They are particularly suited for use in cold waters and can be uncomfortable to wear in hot climates unless the membrane material has breathable properties. Buy ones that are oversize to allow for warm polyester underclothes and ease of movement. Then they are also easy to get on and off.

The drysuit is a one-piece waterproof garment. The drytop is designed to be worn with hi-fit trousers which I find preferable, because you can take the top off when the weather is hot and sultry.

The other priority is a life jacket that will keep you afloat with your head above water in the event of a dunking. Self-inflating

Two types of dry wear for open keelboat sailing. Left: A one-piece suit with rubber seals. Right: A drytop jacket worn in conjunction with hi-fit waterproof trousers.

life jackets are not suitable for use in sailing dinghies because they inflate whenever they get wet, and not just when you fall overboard, but provide an additional safety measure on a yacht.

Lifejackets are available to match all shapes and sizes. They are even available for pets. Make sure that your choice is type-approved by your national standards authority, sized to match your body weight and fits comfortably over your sailing suit.

Lifejackets sold in the European Union are CE tested and approved. In the USA, choose a lifejacket that is type-approved by the United States Coast Guard. Type III flotation aids have 69N (15.5lb/17kg) of buoyant force and include a collar to kee p the face of an unconscious person out of the water.

What to wear offshore

Sailing offshore requires rather more protection than sailing around for a few hours inshore, and the better the clothing, the more you will enjoy it. When you are on an overnight passage or longer, clothing has to keep you warm and dry in the cold of night as well as daytime. If comfort is a priority, then don't skimp on cost. Manufacturers have gone to great lengths to develop 3-layer clothing systems to cope with these climatic extremes.

Staying warm and keeping dry are really two sides of the same coin as far as thermal insulation is concerned. Cotton underclothes for instance can absorb up to 100% of their own weight in water or sweat, and with this moisture next to the skin, body heat is sapped out 30 times faster than with a dry fabric. By

contrast, hollow-fibred, polyester thermal undergarments have the unique ability to wick perspiration away from the skin by capillary action into the outer garments, thus keeping the skin warm and dry. The decks can get very wet and slippery, so good boots with nonslip soles are another priority.

Personal protection
- Wear enough clothes to keep warm.
- Always have sufficient protection from the sun, and wear good quality sunglasses.
- Always wear footwear with closed toes when outside the cockpit. There are many trip hazards on the deck and it is all too easy to injure yourself.

Safety gear

The golden rule on any vessel is to keep one hand for the yacht...and one for yourself. The latest self-inflating lifejackets, with all-important crotch straps, will keep you afloat with your head above water indefinitely, but it is far better to avoid falling overboard in the first place.

Life jackets

The best life jackets are those that incorporate a safety harness with a 6ft (2m) line and self-locking quick release carbine hooks at each end for you to attach to jack stays running either side of the deck and across the cockpit.

It is a good rule to insist that crew members always wear their life jacket whenever they don their oilskins and clip on their harnesses as they come out of the companionway. A good decision rule is when <u>not</u> to wear a life jacket, rather than when to wear it.

Make sure that your choice of life jacket is type-approved by your national standards authority, sized to match your body weight, and fits comfortably over your sailing suit.

The life jacket should have a minimum buoyancy of 150 Newtons, and should be tested when first purchased by being inflated orally and left for a period, and then annually. Keep spare gas canisters onboard. The skipper must ensure that the crew has been issued with lifejackets / harnesses and instructed on their use before going to sea. Whilst at sea, the crew shall wear lifejackets:

• when the skipper requests;

Left: A self-inflating life jacket for use on open keelboats and yachts.
Right: A buoyancy aid for dinghy sailing.

• on deck at night;
• in fog;
• when the mainsail is reefed;
• in more than 10 kts apparent wind when flying a spinnaker;
• when in the harness being suspended off the deck;
• if the individual wants to;
• if the individual is a nonswimmer;
• in the boat.

Use of lifelines

Lifelines shall ALWAYS be worn with lifejackets. A lifeline attached to a jackstay will keep you connected to the yacht in the event of you falling overboard.

An offshore life jacket fitted with crotch straps, harness and lifelines.

Whilst at sea, the crew shall clip on as follows:

- At night.
- During the day when conditions warrant the use of lifejackets.
- Before coming up on deck at night.
- Where possible clip on at the high side.
- Only clip on to the jack stays and the dedicated strong points, never to the standing rigging.

Other personal safety equipment to be kept ready to hand in the pockets of your oilskins are:

- knife or multi-purpose tool;
- LED flashlight;
- whistle;
- personal man-overboard beacon (MOB) if the yacht is equipped with a MOB receiver;
- orange smoke flare.

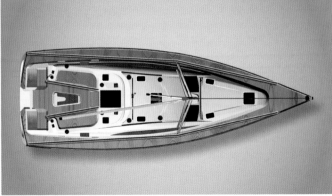

Permanent jack stays highlighted in red should run the length of the deck and cockpit for the crew to clip onto. (left) Strong points in the cockpit allow the crew to click on as they come out of the companionway.

Essential equipment

After checking your own protective clothing and buoyancy aid, the open keelboat should have a safety check before setting sail.

Outboard stowed securely with sufficient fuel to get you home.

Safety equipment
Anchor and line. A folding anchor takes up least space. Together with the anchor line, which can double as a towing warp, pack at least 5ft (1.5m) of chain to act as ground tackle to hold the anchor down. These must be stowed securely to prevent them falling out in the event of a broach.

The anchor line/tow rope should be at least three times the length of the keelboat and with a minimum breaking strain of twice the weight of the boat and crew.

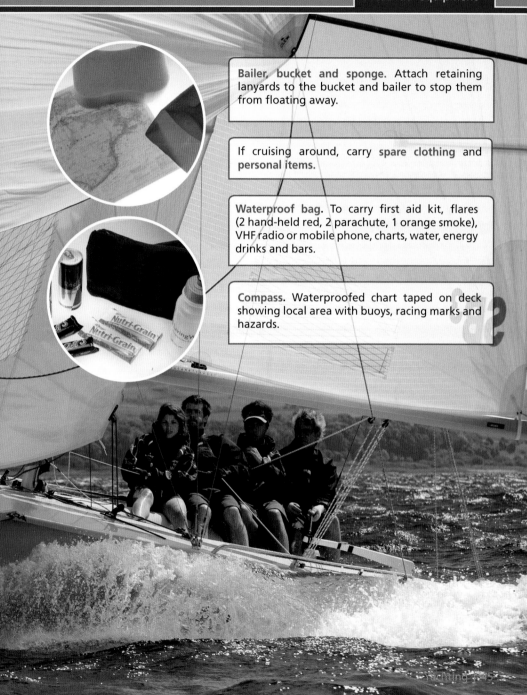

Bailer, bucket and sponge. Attach retaining lanyards to the bucket and bailer to stop them from floating away.

If cruising around, carry spare clothing and personal items.

Waterproof bag. To carry first aid kit, flares (2 hand-held red, 2 parachute, 1 orange smoke), VHF radio or mobile phone, charts, water, energy drinks and bars.

Compass. Waterproofed chart taped on deck showing local area with buoys, racing marks and hazards.

Offshore safety equipment checklist

Distress flares
2 orange smoke hand flares
2 white hand flares
4 red parachute rockets
6 red hand flares

Dan buoy attached to lifebuoy
with light, whistle and drogue attached

Emergency Position Indicating Radio Beacon
(EPIRB) if doing significant offshore sailing

Search & Rescue Transponder (SART) if
doing significant offshore sailing

2 buckets with lanyards attached to handles

2 x bilge pumps (manual and electric) – the
manual one should operate from the cockpit

Radar reflector (an active radar transponder
provides best visibility to other vessels)

Fog horn + spare cannisters

Spare fuel, oil and water (10ltrs of each + funnel)

Liferaft (serviced annually)

Anchor ball + motoring cone

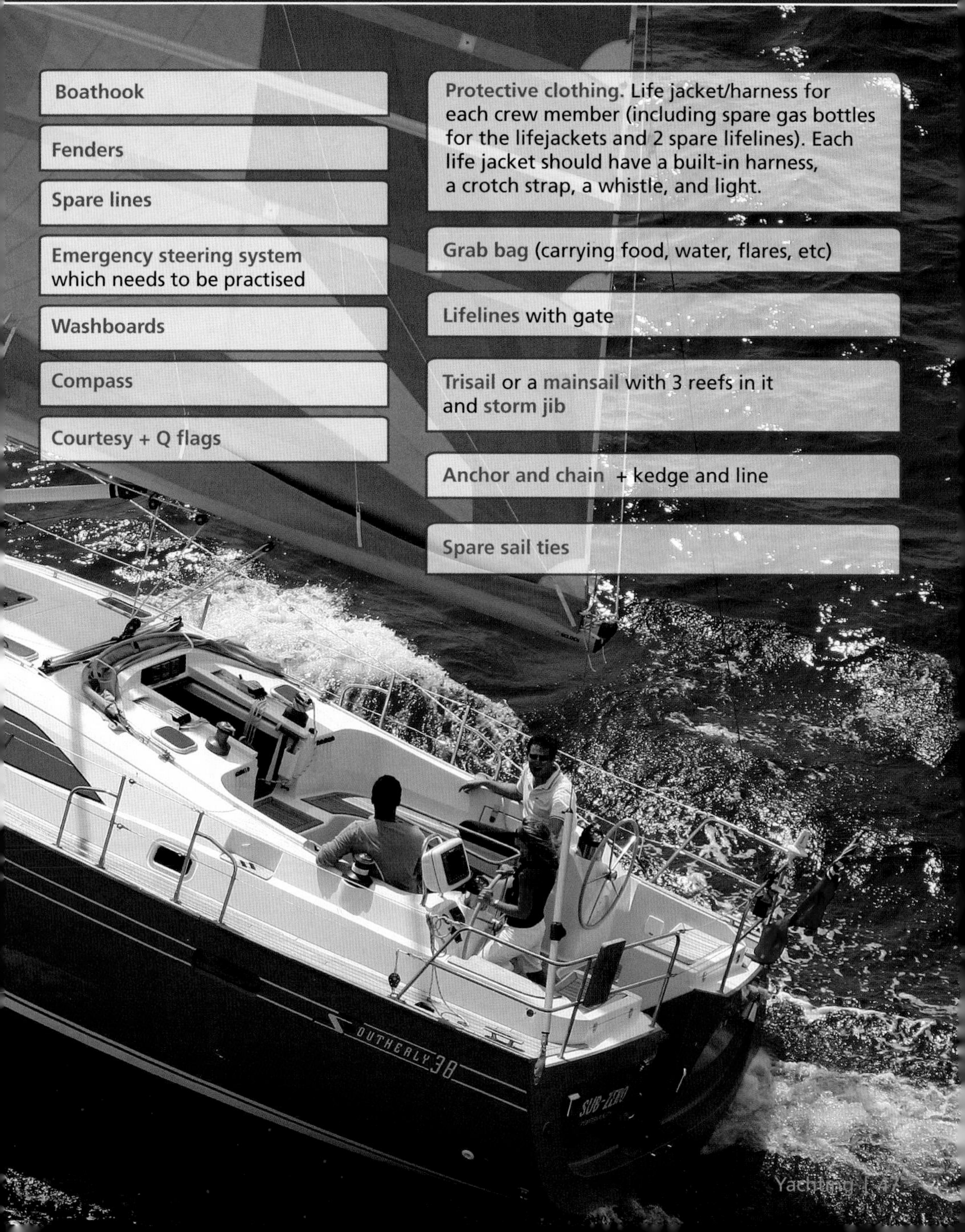

Boathook

Fenders

Spare lines

Emergency steering system which needs to be practised

Washboards

Compass

Courtesy + Q flags

Protective clothing. Life jacket/harness for each crew member (including spare gas bottles for the lifejackets and 2 spare lifelines). Each life jacket should have a built-in harness, a crotch strap, a whistle, and light.

Grab bag (carrying food, water, flares, etc)

Lifelines with gate

Trisail or a mainsail with 3 reefs in it and storm jib

Anchor and chain + kedge and line

Spare sail ties

Onboard safety checklist

Tool kit
- Bolt croppers
- Bosun's chair
- Adjustable wrench
- Cable ties
- Centre punch
- Electrical crimping tool + connectors
- Electrical tape
- Emery cloth or boards
- Epoxy rapid cement
- Gasket cement
- Hammer
- Hand drill
- Hose clips
- Junior hacksaw
- Long nose pliers
- Mole grips
- Plastic piping
- Punch
- Round file
- Rubber mallet
- Set of allen keys
- Set of drill bits
- Set of flat head screwdrivers
- Set of Phillips screwdrivers
- Set of spanners
- Socket set
- Stanley knife
- Spare alternator belt
- Spare batteries
- Spare bulbs and fuses for nav lights and torches
- Spare engine oil filters
- Spare fuel filters
- Spare water pump filter
- Spare water pump belt
- Spare water pump impeller
- Tape measure
- Vernier callipers
- Waterproof grease
- Wire brush

Sail repair kit
- Duck tape
- Fid
- Mousing wire
- Needles
- Sail repair tape
- Sailmaker's palm
- Spare shackles
- Whipping twine

Galley
- Fire blanket
- Safety strop

Fire extinguishers in each cabin and remote controlled extinguisher in engine compartment
Fire blanket within easy reach of galley
Powerful searchlight

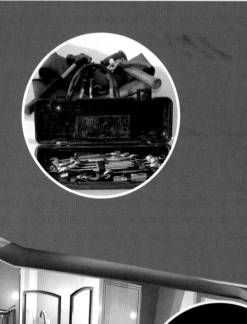

Nav station
- Admiralty list of lights
- Admiralty radio signals
- Almanac
- Back-up radio receiver (wind up)
- Barometer
- Binoculars
- Boat data file
- Breton plotter
- Calculator
- Current charts for region
- Dividers
- Echo sounder
- Emergency torch (wind up)
- Eraser
- GPS
- Log book
- Hand-bearing compass
- Mobile phone + charger
- Oldis lamp
- Pencils and sharpener
- Pilot books + tidal atlas
- Portable VHF + charger + emergency aerial
- Symbols and abbreviations chart

First aid kit + manual
The longer the passage, the better stocked the first aid box should be.
- When day sailing inshore, a simple domestic first aid kit, will suffice, when stored in a waterproof container. If you are planning a weekend or week-long voyage, more comprehensive emergency medical supplies are required.

Getting onboard from dinghy and dock

Dinghies

Tenders are just as their name describes – tippy. Always wear a buoyancy aid before getting in one, and always step into the centre of the dinghy, never on the side. Let the rower position themselves amidships first before loading the bow and stern.

Never overload the dinghy. Make two trips if necessary, the first with people, and the second to carry the stores.

Always shine a light at night to alert other vessels to your position and carry a small anchor and line.

Yachts

Modern designs like the Southerly 38 have a boarding/bathing platform in the stern, which make it easier to get on and off the yacht.

Secure the dinghy side-on to the stern of the yacht using bow and stern lines, and always step out from the centre of the dinghy, and never the gunwale.

When there is a swell running, the gunwale of the dinghy can become trapped under the transom, so moor the dinghy alongside and not at the stern.

Boarding yachts without a transom step is made easier by using removable steps that by hang over the gunwale.

Alternatively tie the dinghy forward so that it lies alongside the shrouds and use the stays to pull yourself up onto the stern gunwale before stepping over the lifelines.

Never pull yourself up on the lifelines or stanchion posts because your weight can loosen the toe rail fastenings and lead to leaks. When stepping aboard from the dock, use the gate (if there is one) within the lifelines by opening the pelican hooks and steady yourself with your hands on the reinforced stanchions.

If there is no gate, then put one foot on the gunwale and grab hold of the cap shroud to pull yourself up and <u>not</u> the lifelines or stanchions.

Replace the gate lines and secure the pelican hooks once onboard.

Rules of the road

All vessels, from the smallest rowing tender to the largest supertanker, are governed by the same rules, known as the International Regulations for Preventing Collisions at Sea or IRPCS. These 'Rules of the Road' take precedence over the International Yacht Racing Rules set by the International Sailing Federation (ISAF). Under the racing rules, vessels not racing are considered obstructions to be avoided using the IRPCS. So if you don't obey the rules, your competitors can protest you out of the race for offences against an innocent bystander!

The IRPCS are published in many forms, and for the price of a beer you can pick up a back pocket-sized copy at any nautical bookstore – this is strongly recommended for any skipper.

The IRPCS cover all aspects and scenarios of vessel interaction at sea. These are summarised by Rule 2, which makes law the application of good seamanship above the blind following of the later Rules – in other words to avoid immediate danger, a departure from the Rules may be necessary.

Rule 3 defines vessel types and nautical terms. In particular, a power driven vessel is defined as one propelled by machinery, e.g. a yacht motor-sailing.

Rule 5 dictates that a proper lookout should be kept at all times by sight and hearing, as well as by all other means appropriate, e.g. using radar correctly in restricted visibility.

One of the most common ways for a yacht to get in trouble is to be going too fast for the circumstances. All the factors that affect a yacht's safe speed are detailed in Rule 6. These come down to common sense and the awareness of where you are and what is around you. Very importantly it mentions the limitations of radar equipment – just because a yacht is fitted with radar there is no guarantee that it is working properly or that the operator knows what he or she is doing! Radar assisted collisions are caused by the incorrect use of radar information – if you don't know how to interpret it, don't assume it will magically keep you safe in restricted visibility.

The assessment of whether a risk of collision exists or not is discussed in Rule 7. This also mentions the dangers of scanty radar information! If an approaching vessel is on a reasonably constant bearing, then there is such a risk – this bearing can be checked using a compass, or by lining the approaching vessel up with a stanchion, for example. In confined waters with large vessels, make sure that you

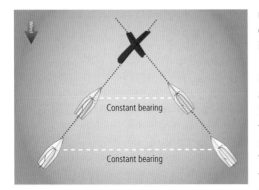

Constant bearing

Constant bearing

look at the entire length of the other vessel – on occasions, if the bow doesn't get you the stern will.

Rule 8 outlines action to avoid collision. The fundamentals are that this action should be early, easily visible to the other vessel and with due regard to the observance of good seamanship. You can change either or both of your speed and heading, and if you're doing so at night make sure you show the other vessel a different aspect light. Importantly, if you happen to be the stand-on vessel, you need to watch the oncoming vessel carefully and if

necessary take avoiding action yourself if you cannot see any change. This is also emphasised in Rule 16.

Rule 9 governs what to do if you meet a large vessel in a narrow channel or harbour, and requires vessels of less than 65.6ft (20m) in length and sailing vessels not to impede the passage of a vessel which can safely navigate only within such a narrow channel. Think about your actions early in relation to the wind direction, tide or current flow and other vessels in your area. Options may include timing your entrance to the harbour so as to miss the shipping, sailing alongside, picking up a mooring till the traffic has passed, sailing into shallow water or out of the main channel, or even just turning around and sailing away from the danger. One classic mistake is to get too close to the bow of an oncoming vessel, forcing them out into the channel and trapping you between them and the side of the harbour. Remember that not all power boaters are aware of the mechanics of tacking upwind and don't understand why you are zigzagging in front of them.

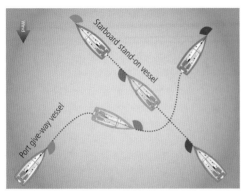

Starboard stand-on vessel

Port give-way vessel

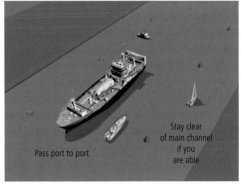

Pass port to port

Stay clear of main channel if you are able

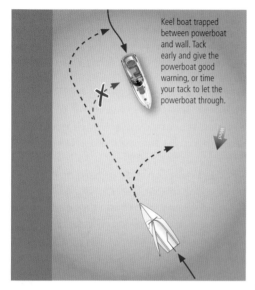

Keel boat trapped between powerboat and wall. Tack early and give the powerboat good warning, or time your tack to let the powerboat through.

Harbour authorities may have local bylaws which supersede the IRPCS inside their jurisdiction, such as allowing fishing boats to trawl in the harbour, banning the use of spinnakers, or giving commercial shipping absolute rights over all types of pleasure craft. However, such special rules should conform as closely as possible to the IPRCS and it is important to get the relevant information from the harbour office or harbour master's staff before setting out.

Rule 10 covers Traffic Separation Schemes, essentially highways for shipping in open waters. They control the movement of vessels in congested areas by regulating opposing flows. Traffic Separation Schemes are divided into three areas:

- Inshore Traffic Zones on either side of the two highways can be used by vessels less than 65.6ft (20m) or sailing vessels. They are also frequently used by fishing vessels when fishing. Large vessels may also use an inshore traffic zone when en route to a port or to avoid immediate danger.
- Traffic Lanes are normally 3 miles (5km) wide or more. These lanes are usually used only by larger vessels. If you enter one of these lanes, do so at a shallow angle to filter in with the flow of traffic and do not impede the safe passage of any shipping.
- The Separation Zone is the central reservation dividing the two traffic lanes (the 'purple patch' on Admiralty charts). Small vessels may only use the separation lanes when crossing the area.

Rules of the road for vessels less than 65.6ft (20m) or sailing vessels are as follows:
- Whenever possible stay away from the Traffic Lanes; use the Inshore Traffic Zone.
- You shall not impede vessels using the Traffic Lanes.
- If you have to cross the lanes then do so with your heading at right angles to the traffic flow.

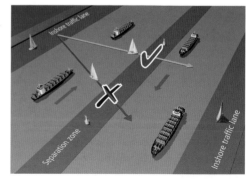

The remaining rules govern how vessels interact with each other, starting with Rule 12 which specifically discusses sailing vessels. There are three things to remember:

- A yacht on PORT tack gives way to a yacht on STARBOARD tack.
- If both yachts are on the same tack then the windward yacht gives way to the leeward yacht.
- If you are on PORT tack and unsure of the other vessel, then give way anyway.

One easy reminder as to which tack you are on is to mark the boom where the helm can see it clearly. Inscribe with an indelible pen on the left hand side of the boom PORT and on the right hand side STARBOARD. Alternatively, place a red sticker on the port side, and a green one on the starboard side.

An overtaking vessel must keep clear of the slower vessel until they are past and clear. Rule 13 defines you to be overtaking if you are coming up on another vessel from an angle more than 22.5° abaft her beam. In other words, if you are approaching her and can only see her stern light. It doesn't matter whether you are a sailing yacht overtaking a powerboat – as the overtaking vessel you must stay clear.

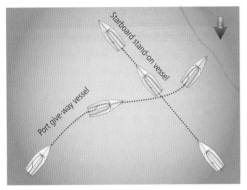

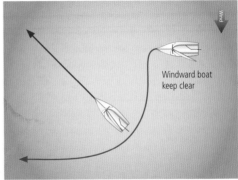

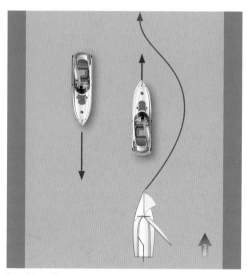

Overtaking sailboat must not impede other vessels that may be constrained by the channel.

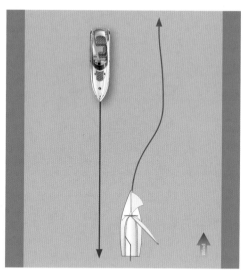

Pass port to port and keep to the correct side of the channel. Where the motor vessel is constrained by the channel, the sailboat has a responsibility to stay well clear.

An obvious collision situation is the Head on Situation. Rule 14 applies when you are under power, and you should alter course to starboard to avoid the collision. Remember, if both vessels are sailing this doesn't apply. Here, the sailing rules given in Rule 12 govern your actions.

When a Crossing Situation under power occurs, Rule 15 tells us that the vessel which has the other on her starboard side is the give-way vessel, and should take avoiding action to avoid crossing ahead of the other vessel, generally by altering course to starboard and passing behind her. A good way of remembering this is to think of the navigation light that you would see – green means go, red means stop.

All these rules have spoken about the actions of the give-way vessel. The stand-on vessel also has responsibilities, detailed in Rule 17, to keep your course and speed, but be ready to take avoiding action if necessary.

Rule 18 defines the pecking order of who should give way to whom. Sailing vessels are generally required to keep out of the way of vessels not under command, restricted in their ability to manoeuvre, or engaged in fishing. See the list of vessels opposite that sailing boats must give way to and the shapes or flags that tell us why.

Navigation in Restricted Visibility is a much misunderstood rule. Rule 19 covers this, and it is vital to understand that the rules describing vessel interaction (Rules 12 through to 18) do not apply when the visibility is such that the vessels are not in sight of each other. It boils down to a few important points:

- Proceed at a safe speed so you can manoeuvre easily.
- If you detect another vessel by radar alone and you determine that a risk of collision exists, then take avoiding action as early as possible. There is no set option, but avoid turning to port for a vessel forward of the beam, and avoid a course alteration towards a vessel on or abaft the beam. Often the easiest option is to slow right down early on, or stop if you are not sure of the situation.
- Without radar: if you hear a vessel forward of the beam, then slow right down while still keeping steerage, and be extremely cautious until the risk has passed.

Shipping

Keep a watchful eye open for ships. Their speed can be very deceptive. Even in restricted waters, these vessels can be making as much as 15 knots in order to keep steerage way during turns. That means they will be bearing down on you at the rate of 1 mile every 4 minutes, so a ship that was on the horizon one minute can be a real hazard within 10-15 minutes. Ships may also be constrained to the deep-water channel and unable to alter course to avoid you. Remember that visibility from the ship's bridge is very restricted. A small yacht will often 'disappear' from the view of the pilot and helm when more then half a mile ahead, so don't even consider crossing ahead unless you are absolutely sure you can get across in time. When crossing a channel, sail well within your personal limits. Large vessels will generate a temporary wind shadow, so be aware and prepared should you lose sail

power when the ship passes by. Commercial ships are busy earning a living. Sailors, on the other hand, are out there for enjoyment, so be considerate, keep well out of the way and abide by the rules.

Fishing/Trawling	
Restricted in ability to manoeuvre Both of the above will be moving slowly.	
Constrained by Draught The big boats will stay inside the buoyed channel.	
Not under Command Rare near the coast.	
Underwater Operations Dredging or pipe laying. Probably stationary or moving very slowly.	
Diving. Dive boats fly flag **Alpha**. Keep well clear to avoid divers 'popping up' in front of you.	
Work boats can fly the flags **Romeo Yankee** which mean: 'Pass me slowly - no wash'.	

Sound signals

Powerboats are fond of making sound signals as it is easy for them – they just press a button. Sailors in open keelboats normally don't have the signalling equipment necessary to

draw attention to themselves, and can only communicate their intentions by using bold manoeuvres in good time.

The sound signals you are most likely to hear will be short (•) or long (–) blasts. Long tends to be more than 4 seconds.

•	I am turning to starboard.
••	I am turning to port.
•••	I am slowing down or going backwards.
•••••	I am unclear of your intentions (and getting worried).
–	I am coming (possibly round a corner or under a bridge).

✓ Make your alteration in course early and obvious.

✓ Pass at a safe distance.

✓ If the ship gives five short blasts they are already worried about what you are doing.

✓ Avoid collisions at all costs.

✓ Use common sense.

✓ Port gives way to starboard.

✓ Windward boat keeps clear.

✓ Overtaking boat keeps clear.

✓ Treat shipping with respect.

Sailing vessels under power

By night

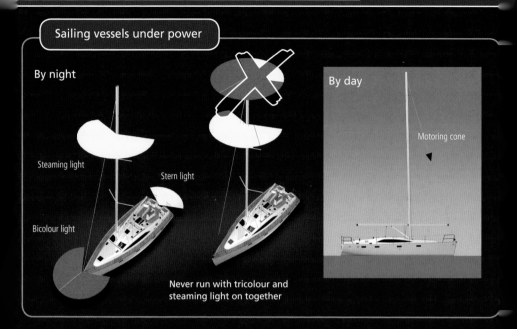

Steaming light

Stern light

Bicolour light

By day

Motoring cone

Never run with tricolour and
steaming light on together

Under sail

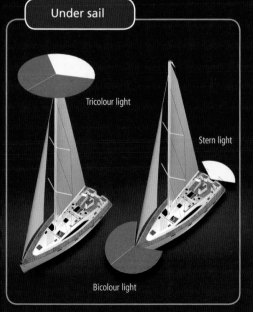

Tricolour light

Stern light

Bicolour light

Power vessels

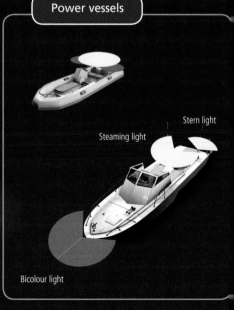

Stern light

Steaming light

Bicolour light

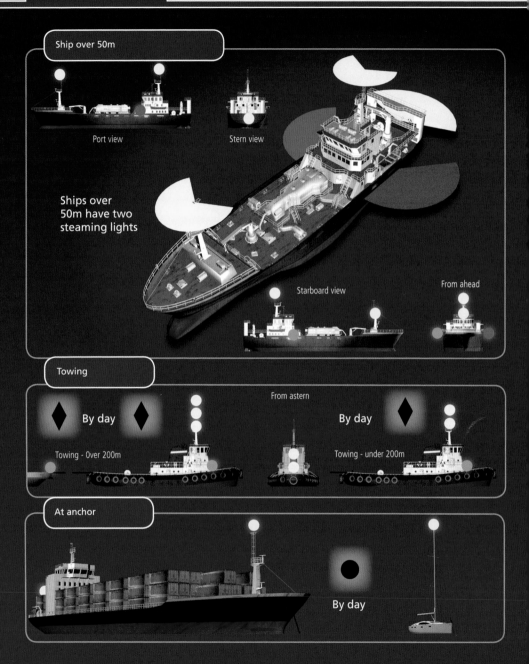

Ship over 50m

Port view

Stern view

Ships over
50m have two
steaming lights

Starboard view

From ahead

Towing

By day

From astern

By day

Towing - Over 200m

Towing - under 200m

At anchor

By day

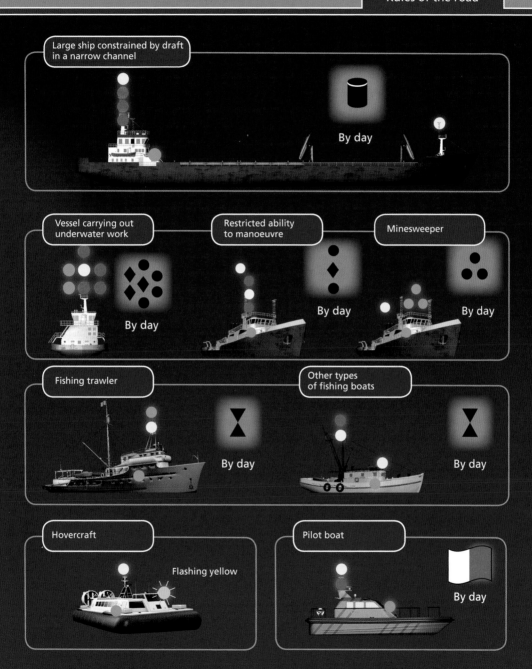

Large ship constrained by draft in a narrow channel

By day

Vessel carrying out underwater work

By day

Restricted ability to manoeuvre

By day

Minesweeper

By day

Fishing trawler

By day

Other types of fishing boats

By day

Hovercraft

Flashing yellow

Pilot boat

By day

Bending on sails, roller furling and reefing

On many yachts, the mainsail is stowed permanently on the boom and protected with a cover, and the headsail is roller furled on the headstay ready for a quick get-away. On more traditional yachts, the headsails are hanked to the headstay, and on racing yachts a headfoil, invariably with two tracks to allow for a second sail to be hoisted before pulling down the first, requires headsails fitted with a bolt rope to slide up the track.

Mainsail

❶ Start with the clew and feed the bolt rope into the boom track opening near to the mast. One person then feeds the bolt rope into the track while the other pulls the clew out towards the end of the boom.

❷ Once the foot of the mainsail is in the track, the person at the mast connects the tack of the sail to the shackle attached to the inboard end of the boom.

❸ Some yachts are equipped with loose-footed mainsails, which should be attached by the tack, and then by the clew to the outhaul. If there is a separate outhaul line running through the boom to a cleat, this is attached by shackling it to the clew as in this picture. The outhaul is now pulled out until the foot is under slight tension. Where there is no outhaul, this is achieved by lacing the clew outhaul line through the boom end and clew several times and pulling tight, and tying it off with two half hitches.

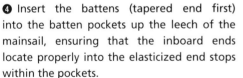

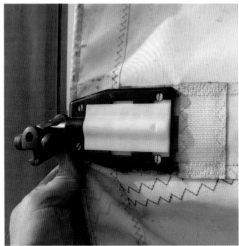

❹ Insert the battens (tapered end first) into the batten pockets up the leech of the mainsail, ensuring that the inboard ends locate properly into the elasticized end stops within the pockets.

❺ With full length battens, ensure that the end fits slots into the inboard fitting attached to the luff.

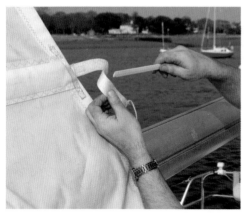 

❻ The outboard ends must also be pushed well down into the pocket opening.

❼ If the mainsail is to remain bent on the boom, then consider having Velcro strips that are fed inside the pocket with a prodder to secure to the battens in place.

 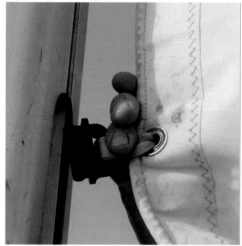

❽ and **❾** To hoist mainsail, turn the yacht head to wind and attach halyard to headboard. Raise the sail gradually, inserting the luff sail slides into the mast luff track as the sail goes up. Once the sail is hoisted, lock off the mast luff track to retain the sail slides within the mast when the sail is lowered.

Headsails

Hanked headsails

Ask the skipper to select the headsail most suitable for the conditions. Bring this up on deck and carry it to the bows. Attach the headsail tack to the bow fitting and put a tie around the sail to keep it together.

Then run your hands up the luff attaching the spring hanks to the headstay as you go, ensuring that they all face the same way and none are clipped on upside down, which will cause a twist in the sail.

If the headsail is to be hoisted immediately, then attach the halyard to the head of the sail making sure it is temporarily secured to the pulpit.... and tie the sheets to the clew using bowlines, unless they are attached with shackles.

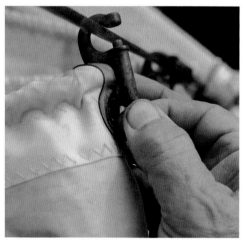

If the headsail is to be stowed ready for hoisting at a later stage, then secure the sail with a sail tie to the toe rail and shackle the halyard to the pulpit.

Headsail sheet is led to an adjustable fairlead block attached to a track on the side deck, then up to the primary winch.

Headsail sheets

With large overlapping headsails set on masthead rigged and some fractionally rigged yachts, the sheets will run outboard of the shrouds and through adjustable fairlead blocks attached to tracks running fore and aft up the side deck, or to blocks attached to the toe rail before being led (sometimes via turning blocks) to the primary winches on either side of the cockpit.

Tie a stopper knot in the end of each sheet to prevent the ropes from running back through the fairleads.

With short overlapped, self-tacking headsails like those fitted on the fractionally rigged Southerly 38, a single sheet, often wire with a rope tail, is already rigged through a block attached to a transverse track forward of the mast.

Simply shackle the free end of the sheet to the clew of the sail. The working end passes through a conduit within the deck to a single winch mounted for that purpose.

Using winches

The first practical step for the sailing novice is to understand the huge loadings that occur on sheets and halyards once a sail has the wind in it. Even on relatively small yachts like my own 27ft (9m) *Sea Jay*, it is futile to attempt to pull in a genoa sheet or take the strain on a halyard without some form of mechanical advantage. This is where the winch comes in, providing the mechanical advantage to tension and release the loadings on sheets and halyards. There are two types: the standard and the self-tailing winch.

Both operate in a clockwise motion, though some larger versions can have two or more gears which engage when the handle rotation is reversed.

Self-tailing winch

This Southerly 42 RS is equipped with a self-tacking jib with the single sheet led to track running athwartships across the foredeck.

Standard winch

❶ Standard winch – 2-man operation

Tailer: Applies two turns clockwise around the winch.

❷ Tailer: Pulls in the rope to take up the slack, then, maintaining pressure on the rope, fills the drum, usually with three or four turns, depending on the size of the line.

Grinder: Slots the handle in place while the tailer maintains tension on the rope. Using both hands, turns the handle clockwise with shoulder centred over the winch for maximum effect.

❸ Tailer: Must maintain constant pressure on the rope end to stop slippage around the winch and keep hands clear of the handle sweep.

Tailer: Also calls the shots, calling 'Sheet' for more or 'Stop' when fine-tuning tension at the end of the process. Once the winding is complete, the tailer cleats the rope end using the OXO method for quick release, and the grinder removes and stows the handle. For quick release, simply undo the rope around the cleat and pull the tail up to free the coils around the winch.

Self-tailing winch – 1-man operation

Apply two turns clockwise around the winch. Pull in the rope to take up the slack, then, maintaining pressure on the rope, load the drum with an extra turn before passing the tail over the guide bar and into the grooved, spring-loaded, circular jaws on the top of the winch.

Slot the handle in place and, using both hands if necessary, turn the handle clockwise, with your shoulder centred over the winch for maximum effect. Once the winding is complete, give a tug on the tail to ensure that the rope is locked within circular jaws, remove the handle and stow it away, and put two safety turns around the winch to prevent the line accidently being knocked out of the jaws.

Connections

Shackles must always be done up tight otherwise they will unscrew themselves at the most awkward moments. That leads to the premise that they will be difficult to undo, so have a shackle key (or pliers) in your pocket or on a lanyard ready to hand.

Key shackles, which have a captive pin and quick release to save you from fumbling with cold fingers and dropping the pin overboard, can be considered for lighter loaded connections.

Snap shackles are quick-release connectors used to connect halyards and spinnaker sheets to sails. The release plunger should have a short lanyard or loop attached to release the shackle when under load.

A snatch block is often used as a temporary sheet block. Fitted with a quick-release snap shackle, it can be attached to the toe rail or deck eye, and the block can be opened and the rope laid in it, even under load, without the need to undo the working end to thread it through.

To release, simply release the safety turns, pull the rope out of the circular jaws and pull up to free the coils around the winch.

To ease the sheet a small amount on either type of winch, release the tail with one hand and press the palm of your other hand against the coils around the winch.

You can then control the gradual release of the rope.

Captive key shackle.

Snap shackle.

Snatch block opened to accept line...

... and closed.

Clearing a riding turn

A riding turn occurs when one or more coils become crossed and lock around the winch. This can happen when too many turns have been applied to the winch before the slack has been pulled in, or the lie of the rope is at the wrong angle to the winch drum.

To clear the locked rope, take a spare line and tie a rolling hitch to the loaded line leading back to the winch. Lead the working end, via a snatch or turning block, to another winch and transfer the load.

With the load removed from the riding turn, it is now easy to release the snagged coils. Reload the winch and take up the tension on the original line, then release the spare line.

Clearing a riding turn. Temporary sheet tied to the genoa sheet with a rolling hitch and led back to a second winch via a snatch block. This is used to relieve pressure on the genoa sheet and allow the riding turn to be cleared from the winch.

Reefing

Yachts are designed to sail upwind at 15-20° of heel. Once the toe rail is kissing the water, it is time to reef the sails because the boat is heeled over too far for the keel to be effective in limiting leeway.

This involves reducing the area of the headsail and mainsail in proportion to each other in order to maintain the same vertical position for the centre of effort and keep the boat balanced. If you simply reduce headsail area, the centre of effort will move aft and the yacht will exhibit heavy weather helm (heavy to steer) and have a tendency to point up into wind. If mainsail area is reduced alone, then the opposite occurs: the steering will become light (lee helm) and the yacht will have a tendency to bear away from the wind.

Stage 1
As wind levels begin to increase, start by rolling in a few turns on the headsail or changing down from genoa to working jib.

Stage 2
Take in first reef in mainsail.

Stage 3
Reduce headsail size to half and take in 2nd reef in mainsail. Reduce headsail size to 1/3 and take in 3rd reef in mainsail.

Headsail unfurled.

Headsail ⅓ furled.

Headsail fully furled.

Roller furling

On some yachts, the headsail, and sometimes the mainsail, is bent permanently onto the rig, to simplify sail handling and reefing. The convenience with all these systems is that they can be controlled from the cockpit without the need to go up on deck (unless something goes wrong!).

In-mast mainsail furling system.

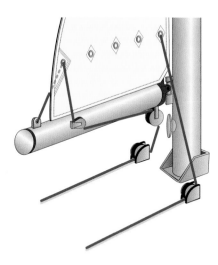

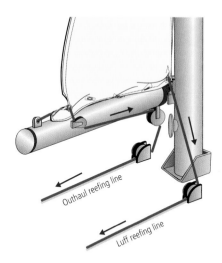

Outhaul reefing line

Luff reefing line

Mainsail slab reefing systems

Slab reefing is the most common method of reefing a mainsail, and when reefing lines and halyards are led back along the coach roof, it is possible to complete the process from within the safety of the cockpit.

❶ Carefully release the vang so the boom can freely move up and down. Ease the mainsheet so the sail is depowered (i.e. flapping) and take up on the topping lift (to stop the boom from falling down below head height).

❷ Release the main halyard and ease it out to bring the first reef cringle down in line with the gooseneck. Tension the inboard reefing line, or hook the cringle on the horn cleat on the gooseneck and re tension the main halyard.

❸ Tension the outboard reefing line to pull the first reef cringle on the leech down to the boom. Release the topping lift, sheet in and re- tension the vang.

❹ Once the sail is trimmed and drawing, with the boom solidly fixed in place by the mainsheet, vang and the drive of the sail, it is now safe to have crew working along the boom. An earring should be tied through the reefing cringle at the clew around the boom in case the reefing line snaps. Also, now is a good time to roll up the fold in the bottom of the sail and secure with temporary lacing around the boom.

The boom/coach roof geometry on some yachts may make this difficult – it is the skipper's decision as to whether the bunt of the sail (the unused slabs hanging beneath the boom) requires tidying up or not. Repeat process to put in 2nd and 3rd reef in mainsail.

Boat handling under power – mooring and anchoring

Handling any sized yacht under power needs practice, preferably in a wide open space, to find out how she behaves going astern, the effect windage has on the hull and, most important, the distance she needs to stop. Entering a narrow marina berth is no time to start learning her foibles. The key to successful manoeuvring under power is to do everything in slow motion without fuss, and approach at a controlled speed.

Prop wash/walk

The wash over the rudder from a quick burst of thrust from the propeller, can have a dramatic effect in spinning the boat round with little forward motion. By giving a series of 'power bursts' fore and aft while holding the helm hard over, the boat can be turned round in a confined area, sometimes within its own length.

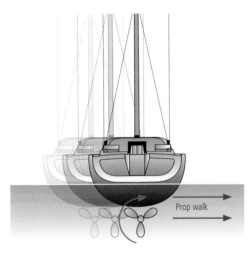

Prop walk

Thrust from the propeller also has a substantial 'paddle wheel' effect on boat handling, and once you know which way it is going to push the stern, this too can be harnessed to work for you in a confined space.

When first putting the engine in gear, the propeller tends to pull the stern sideways in the same direction as its rotation. This is termed 'prop walk'. Thus a clockwise rotating prop will walk the stern to starboard when starting out in forward gear, and to port when engaged in reverse. Test what the natural inclination is for your yacht and plan your entry and exit from the dock to maximize these traits rather than fight them.

When forward gear is engaged, the flow of water from the propeller immediately hits the rudder. This can be used to provide a turning force before the boat is moving at all. With the rudder angled hard over, the prop wash is deflected to one side and pushes the stern round in the opposite direction. Going astern can be another matter though, since the rudder needs water flowing over it to be of any use. As the propeller is now directing water forward round the keel, rather than aft over the rudder, it will not be effective until the boat is making some progress astern. Yachts, like my own traditional long-keeled *Sea Jay*, have a mind of their own when it comes to reversing into a tight spot, but modern designs, with its fin and skeg profile are much more predictable. Other designs fitted with twin rudders like the Southerly are also well mannered when going astern, but because the rudders are not sighted within the flow from the propeller, the twin foils do not generate prop wash. In such cases, a bow thruster is almost essential and makes the whole business of manoeuvring so much easier.

Turning

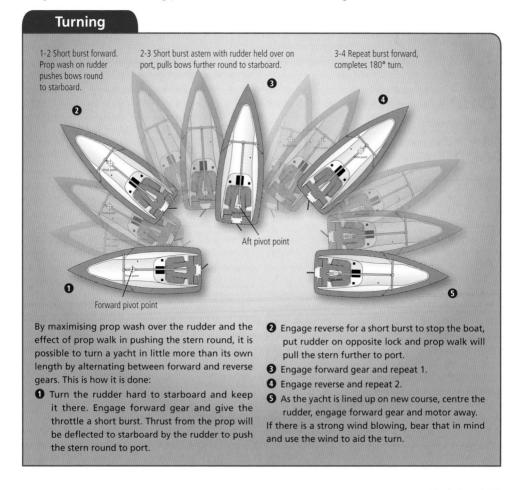

1-2 Short burst forward. Prop wash on rudder pushes bows round to starboard.

2-3 Short burst astern with rudder held over on port, pulls bows further round to starboard.

3-4 Repeat burst forward, completes 180° turn.

Aft pivot point

Forward pivot point

By maximising prop wash over the rudder and the effect of prop walk in pushing the stern round, it is possible to turn a yacht in little more than its own length by alternating between forward and reverse gears. This is how it is done:

1 Turn the rudder hard to starboard and keep it there. Engage forward gear and give the throttle a short burst. Thrust from the prop will be deflected to starboard by the rudder to push the stern round to port.

2 Engage reverse for a short burst to stop the boat, put rudder on opposite lock and prop walk will pull the stern further to port.

3 Engage forward gear and repeat 1.

4 Engage reverse and repeat 2.

5 As the yacht is lined up on new course, centre the rudder, engage forward gear and motor away.

If there is a strong wind blowing, bear that in mind and use the wind to aid the turn.

Fenders

These are used to protect the yacht when moored alongside a pontoon, harbour wall or another vessel.

Deploy them early when preparing the fore and aft mooring lines. At least three should be concentrated around the point of maximum beam amidships and where the yacht might rub against a pile or ladder.

Tie the fender lines with a round turn and two half hitches to the handrail, toe rail or lifelines and set them high enough to protrude above the pontoon.

Have one large roving fender ready to deploy in the event of miscalculation.

When mooring alongside a harbour wall, use a fender board (plank) outboard of the fenders to level out the uneven surface.

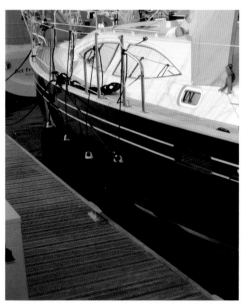

Once the yacht is completely secured, the fenders should be adjusted so that they are all doing a particular job, and secured either from the toe rail (if possible) or from the guardrails at the stanchion posts so as not to drag down the guardrails. Usually they are hung at the same height for aesthetic reasons, but if you are expecting some swell then it may be a good idea to have some hung high and some hung lower than normal in case the boat rolls at the berth.

General notes on mooring

Ideally, each mooring line should be a separate one, and secured to a separate strong point on both the yacht and the pontoon. This ensures that if there is a breakage for some reason the yacht will still be secured by the other lines.

When approaching a berth, the ideal is to be able to stop your yacht in a controlled manner in the correct position so that your crew members can secure the boat to whatever you are aiming for. The two major factors affecting your ability to stop are wind and tide. It is important to know, both by calculation and observation, what affect they are having on the yacht in relation to your berth and to use these combined forces to slow you down.

The tide will ALWAYS move the yacht bodily, and the wind will ALWAYS blow the bow away from it. Make a judgement on which has the stronger effect on the yacht by checking the flow around a marker buoy, and look at the effect the wind is having on vessels tied to swinging moorings, and make your approach into the stream or wind.

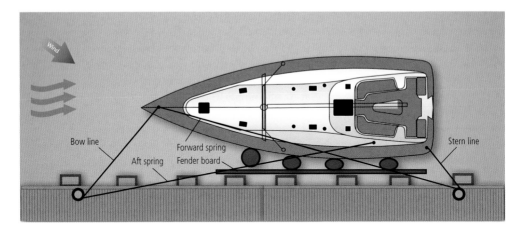

Bow line

Forward spring

Aft spring   Fender board

Stern line

If the weather conditions are not kind to you, there is nothing wrong with asking the marina for help – by having a person on the pontoon to take lines or, if it's really bad, by coming out in a tender to act as a thruster. It is much better to get help and berth safely than not to ask and pile into someone else's pride and joy.

Whenever you are leaving a berth you have three main objectives:

- not to damage any other vessels or facilities;
- not to injure your crew or damage your boat;
- to leave harbour with everyone on board.

A good mental checklist to go through when deciding how to leave the berth is as follows:

- Look at the tidal flow flowing past the yacht, since there may be a local eddy that is different to the overall tidal movement. This tidal flow will bodily move the boat.
- Look at the wind direction and strength – this will blow the bows of your yacht one way or another.

With these observations ask yourself what would happen to the yacht if all your mooring lines were released at the same time. This will allow you to decide which ones are important. For example, if you are moored port side alongside a pontoon, with a one-knot tide coming from bow to stern and a force 3 blowing from 45° on your starboard bow and you suddenly lost all of your lines, then your yacht would be pushed back along the

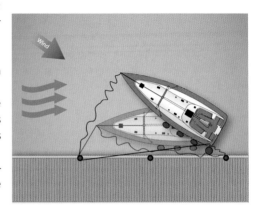

pontoon by the wind. Using this information, you need a line to stop you moving backwards – your stern spring – and a line to control your bow – your bow line. The other two lines are immaterial, and can be removed.

To leave, a fender should be placed at the port quarter and the bow line released, allowing the yacht to sit back upon the stern spring. If the force of the tide is not enough to get the bow through the wind, apply reverse engine power to do so. Once the bow is through the wind, take the engine out of astern, release and recover the spring and drive away from the berth.

vessel later – you will still have the correct number when you leave the harbour!

Most problems encountered when leaving a berth come down to over complicating matters and getting into a tangle. Keep it simple at all times.

Tying up alongside a pontoon
The pontoons and walkways will rise and fall with the tide, so once set, the mooring lines will not need to be adjusted again. The lines used are a bow line, stern line and forward and stern springs which keep the yacht parallel to the pontoon.

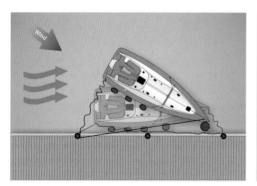

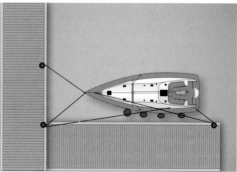

This illustrates the importance of minimising the complexity of the operation – in this case there is no need to have all four lines singled up (i.e. rigged so that they can be pulled in from the yacht). Indeed, you can have a crew member on the pontoon to release the bow line before stepping on board prior to springing off. There is nothing wrong with having a crew member on the pontoon to release lines from an awkward spot, and picking him up from an outer pontoon or

Pile/pontoon berth
Have bow and stern lines rigged on port and starboard sides and boathook at the ready. Approach slowly under power and lasso the windward pile first, then the leeward pile.

- Continue motoring forward to allow bowman to jump ashore.
- Tie up windward bow line first, followed by leeward bow line.

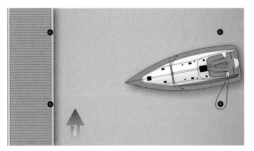

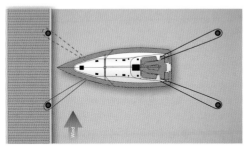

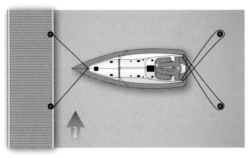

- Cross over the stern lines to act as springs and tension so that bows are just clear of the pontoon or wall.

Depending on whether you prefer to be cockpit facing or away from the pontoon, you may decide to come in stern first. The procedure is exactly the same. In each case, it is vital that the lines lassoing the piles are allowed to run free until the skipper asks for them to be snubbed and made fast.

To leave:

- Set up lines so that they can be pulled through and released from onboard.
- Check which way wind and tide are running and plan departure accordingly.
- Release leeward lines first.
- Release windward bow line and engage reverse (or ahead, if you have entered the berth stern first).
- 'Walk' the yacht aft past the windward pile and release stern line.
- Keep roving fenders at the ready to protect other yachts in the event of drifting down on them.

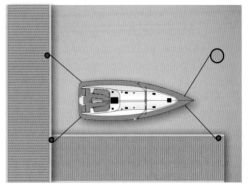

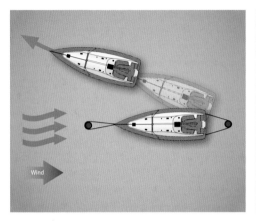

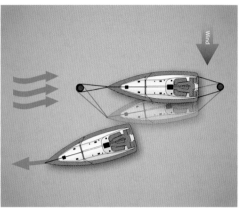

Pile moorings

Have bow and stern lines rigged and boathook at the ready. The stern line should be flaked out so that it cannot snag when running out – this is very important.

- Approach at low speed into tide or wind, whichever is the stronger. If you are unsure, make a dummy run, first into wind and then into the tide to see which has most affect on the yacht.
- As soon as possible, pass the stern line through the stern pile's sliding ring, or preferably attach it if the crewman has time, and let it run free as the yacht carries on.
- As soon as possible, secure the bow line to the sliding ring on the forward pile.

Once the yacht has stopped, ease the bow line gently while taking in the stern line and allow the yacht to settle back to the desired position. Then secure finally as convenient. If conditions are difficult, lasso the stern pile, then the forward pile to secure the boat, then pass lines through the sliding rings and tie off.

To leave:

- Set up lines so that they can be pulled through and released from onboard.
- Head out stern or bow first into the tide. Never attempt to leave down-tide.
- If there is a strong beam wind, head off away from the wind if possible to avoid being blown into the piles.

Mooring alongside a harbour wall

Check with harbour master or pilot notes for rise and fall of tide and any obstructions.

- Always approach into tide or wind, whichever is stronger. Use plenty of fenders to protect hull and use an outer fender board if wall is not of uniform shape.
- Moor up using separate bow/stern lines and springs.
- Warps should be at least three times the rise and fall of tide. If the tidal range is more than 9ft (3m) it may be necessary to have a crew member on board to keep watch over the lines.

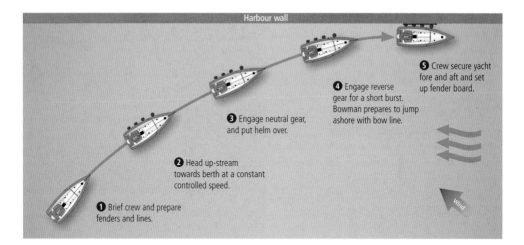

Harbour wall

5 Crew secure yacht fore and aft and set up fender board.

4 Engage reverse gear for a short burst. Bowman prepares to jump ashore with bow line.

3 Engage neutral gear, and put helm over.

2 Head up-stream towards berth at a constant controlled speed.

1 Brief crew and prepare fenders and lines.

Wind

To leave:

- Set up lines so that they can be pulled through and released from onboard.
- Head out stern or bow first into the tide. Never attempt to leave down-tide.
- If space is restricted, hold the down-tide bow/stern line under tension and release the up-tide line, allowing the bow/stern to swing round. Make sure that your vessel cannot move forward or backwards and damage vessels on either side.
- Release the down-tide line when the bow/stern has swung out and motor away

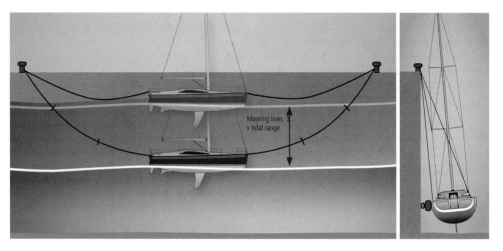

Mooring lines 3 x tidal range

Rafting alongside other boats

Select a boat to come alongside that is of similar or larger size to your own.

- Attach fenders at height to protect both vessels.
- Always approach into tide or wind, whichever is stronger.
- Set up bow/stern lines and springs.
- Ensure that your mast is not in line with mast of the other yacht, otherwise the rigs may clash if there is any swell in the harbour.
- Run shore lines fore and aft to take the strain off the lines of the inside yachts.

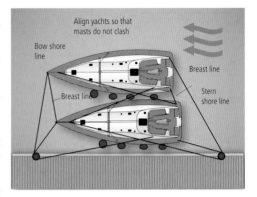

To leave:

- Set up lines so that they can be pulled through and released from onboard.
- Head out stern or bow first into the tide. Never attempt to leave down-tide.
- If space is restricted, hold the down-tide bow/stern line under tension and release the up-tide line, allowing the bow/stern to swing round. Do make sure that your vessel cannot move forward or backwards and damage vessels on either side.
- If you are the inside boat, run the down-tide line of outer yacht around your own yacht and pass to crew member ashore.

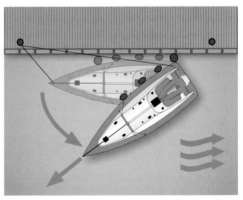

Motor out down tide

Tide will help to set outer vessel back in against the wall or inner yacht.

- Shore side crew member resets shore lines, breast lines and springs.
- Yacht picks up crew member from side of outer vessel.

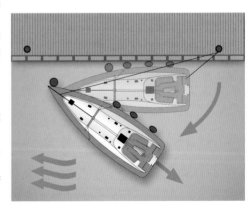

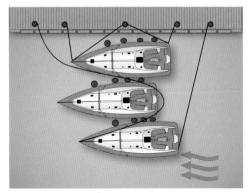

Rafting up on a buoy

Often used in busy harbours as a temporary overnight mooring for visiting yachts.

- Attach fenders at height to protect both vessels.
- Come alongside moored vessel and attach bow line to buoy. The approach direction is given by the other vessel attached to the buoy (assuming she is of a roughly similar type) as she will be directly affected by the combined wind/tide effect at the buoy.
- Attach stern line and springs to moored vessel.
- Ensure that your masts are not going to bang against each other in a swell.

To leave:

- Cast off and leave stern first.
- If in the midst of a group of yachts, run the stern line of one yacht around the bows of your own and attach to vessel on other side.
- Reverse out, leaving one crew member on adjacent yacht to re-tie stern and springs and pick them up from outside yacht.

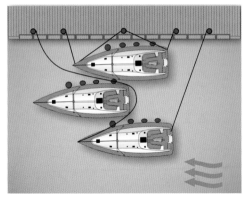

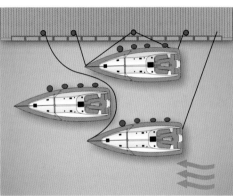

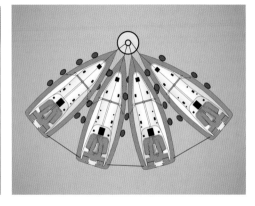

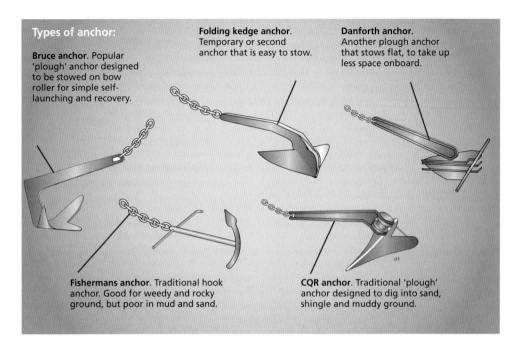

Types of anchor:

Bruce anchor. Popular 'plough' anchor designed to be stowed on bow roller for simple self-launching and recovery.

Folding kedge anchor. Temporary or second anchor that is easy to stow.

Danforth anchor. Another plough anchor that stows flat, to take up less space onboard.

Fishermans anchor. Traditional hook anchor. Good for weedy and rocky ground, but poor in mud and sand.

CQR anchor. Traditional 'plough' anchor designed to dig into sand, shingle and muddy ground.

Tripping line

It is so easy for the anchor to snag on a rock or obstruction – and just as easy to release if a tripping line was set up beforehand. Simply tie a line to the crown of the anchor, and attach a buoy or fender to the other end as a float. Then if the anchor snags, you motor up to the line and pull it onboard to retrieve the anchor upside down.

If a tripping line was not fitted, another way to release the anchor is to motor around and use the power of the vessel to pull the anchor from the opposite direction. If that fails, you have the choice of either diving down to try and release the anchor, or cutting the anchor line.

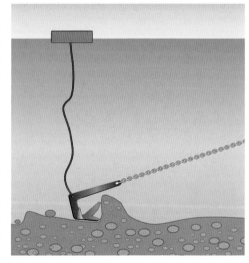

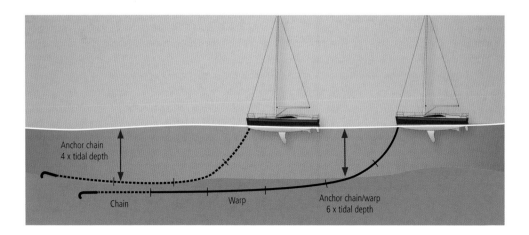

Anchor chain
4 x tidal depth

Chain

Warp

Anchor chain/warp
6 x tidal depth

Anchors work best when the pull is horizontal. The scope of chain deployed needs to be a minimum of 4 times the depth of water - and 6 times the depth when the anchor line is part chain/part warp. The chain is important. The heavier it is, the better you will sleep. Attached to the shank, it keeps the anchor lying horizontal on the bottom and takes some of the 'snatch' out of the line as the yacht rides up and down on the swell. A full-length anchor chain gives most security, but where a rope anchor line is used to save weight, this requires 6-9ft (2-3m) of heavy chain attached to the anchor to weigh it down.

Paint marks on the chain or warp at 6ft (2m) distances provide a visual guide when deploying the anchor.

Using a windlass

The windlass situated on the foredeck is designed to wind the anchor chain. Some windlasses also have a smooth winch drum to control warps. These can be operated manually with a long handle, or are electric or hydraulically powered at the press of a button.

They operate under heavy load, so keep feet, fingers and loose clothing well away.

Choosing an anchorage

Look for good protection from wind and swell. The anchor symbol on the chart is always a good indicator that the bottom is good holding ground. If you have any doubts about the bottom, set up a tripping line to release the anchor should it snag.

- Check the rise and fall of the tide and low water depth on the chart. Is there sufficient water below the keel? When dropping your anchor, use the depth off your echo sounder, not the depth given on the chart – it may have changed!
  Depth required to anchor = desired under keel clearance at low water + height of tide at anchoring – the next low water

- Check rise and fall at the entrance or bar. Will there be sufficient water when you plan to leave?
- Is there sufficient room to swing round with wind or tide?
- Are there any obstructions within this radius? Check by motoring around and monitor the echo sounder.
- Clear the foredeck of sails and prepare the amount of anchor chain and warp needed before dropping anchor:
  Scope required:
  4 x high water depth with chain.
  6 x high water depth with chain and warp.
- Snub the anchor line when fully extended with a short burst of reverse thrust to dig the anchor in.

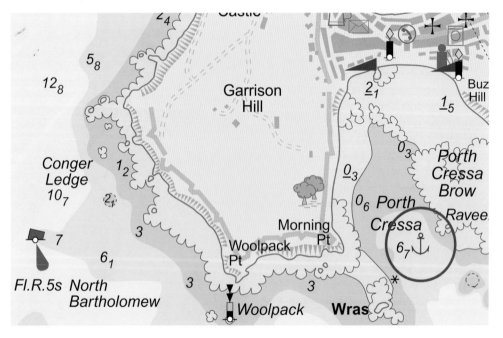

- Check the anchor is not dragging. Take bearings on prominent landmarks and check at 15-minute intervals. You can also tell if the anchor is dragging by testing for vibrations on the anchor line, which will indicate that the anchor is bumping along the bottom.

- If the anchor is dragging, pay out more scope:
  5 x high water depth with chain.
  8 x high water depth with chain and warp.
- If the anchor continues to drag, recover the anchor and select another spot.

Laying two anchors

If bad weather is predicted or you wish to limit the swing of the yacht on the tide or in a crowded anchorage or channel, then these are times to deploy the kedge anchor.

In adverse weather, lay two anchors at 45° to the wind direction on two separate anchor cables set either side of the bows.

Scope required:
5 x high water depth with chain.
8 x high water depth with chain and warp.

To limit swing or maintain a set attitude to the tidal stream, deploy the second (kedge) anchor from the stern.

Clear the stern and prepare the amount of anchor chain and warp needed before dropping anchor.

Scope required:
4 x high water depth with chain.
6 x high water depth with chain and warp.

Pay out the bow anchor line the required distance to drop the stern anchor.

Take up on the bow anchor and cleat off. Snub the stern anchor line by hand to dig the anchor in.

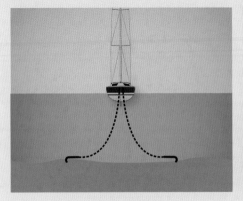
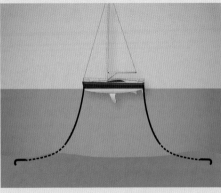

Picking up a mooring

Swing moorings provide a less expensive option to a marina berth. They usually consist of a riser chain linking the main mooring buoy to a heavy sinker or ground chain to which a string of moorings are attached, known as a 'trot'.

If you are lucky, the main mooring buoy will have a pick-up buoy attached to a mooring strop, which is pulled onboard and secured around the bollard on the foredeck.

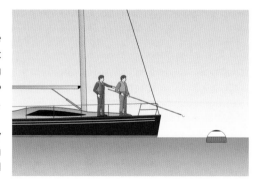

To pick up:

Skipper briefs foredeck crew on approach up-tide or into wind, whichever is stronger.

- Crew has boathook ready and signals angle and distance of buoy to skipper.
- Crew grabs mooring strop with boathook and hauls it up to deck level.
- Second crew member takes hold of pick-up buoy or strop, feeds it through bow roller, passes loop over bollard…
- …and secures the pick-up line using the OXO method around the bollard.

Some commercial moorings do not have a pick-up buoy, but simply an eye through which to attach your own mooring warp.

Bowline coiled and ready…

To pick up:

- Skipper briefs foredeck crew on approach up-tide or into wind.
- Crew has boathook ready and signals angle and distance of buoy to skipper. Second crew has mooring warp and ties off one end on bollard. If conditions allow, crew grabs eye of mooring buoy with boathook…
- ….and second crew member passes mooring warp through eye, brings back through bow roller and ties off on bollard.

If conditions are too rough, one crew member can lasso the buoy with a temporary mooring warp to pull it alongside for a second crewman to attach the mooring warp. Do not leave this lasso on permanently, since it will twist up as the boat swings around the buoy and could damage the mooring.

...to be thrown with both hands to lasso buoy.

Leaving a mooring

Skipper briefs foredeck crew which way he intends to leave.

- Skipper has engine running with propshaft in neutral.
- Skipper calls 'Release mooring' and crew casts off line.
- Skipper allows boat to drift back on tide or wind to avoid running over mooring strop.
- When clear, skipper engages forward gear and steers to clear mooring.

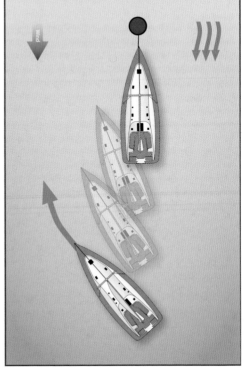

Balance, sail, trim

If you have not taken charge of a boat before, we strongly recommend having an instructor onboard to show you the basics. Choose a day when the winds are moderate and the tidal stream is slack. Start on a beam reach (90° to the wind) with sheets eased halfway out and get the feel of the boat.

The controls

If your yacht has tiller steering like the SB3, then the tiller has to be pushed or pulled in the opposite direction to the way you want to go. If the yacht has wheel steering, then you direct the yacht just as if you are steering a car. The rudder is the primary control.

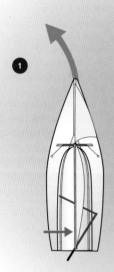  

❶ Push the tiller away from you and the boat will turn up into wind and slow. (This is called luffing up.)

❷ Pull the tiller towards you and the boat will turn away from the wind. (This is termed bearing away.)

❸ Aim the boat at a distant object and practise making a gentle 'S' course towards it. You will soon get the hang of steering.

Balance

On a keelboat like the SB3, it's the job of the crew to balance the boat as well as trim the jib. If the wind is moderate, they will invariably need to sit on the side deck alongside the helm to keep the boat as flat as possible. If the wind drops, then the crew will need to come inboard and sit amidships or even on the leeward side to keep the boat on an even keel.

On larger yachts, crew weight has less impact on righting moment, and though it helps to have the crew lined up on the windward side, reducing sail at the right time is more important to lessen heel and maintain control of the yacht (See reefing sails on page 70)

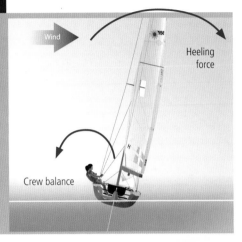

Wind

Heeling force

Crew balance

Stopping

Release the sheets and let the sails right out so they flap.

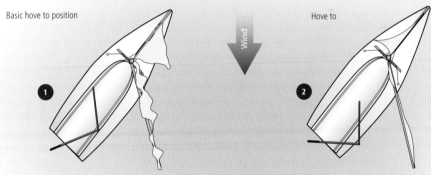

Basic hove to position

Hove to

Wind

1

2

Basic hove to

As the boat slows, the helm steers the bows towards the wind and releases the mainsheet until the sails are empty of wind. Then the helm centres the rudder.

To lie hove to for a longer period, with the boat stable, stopped and quiet, simply pull the headsail in hard on the windward side, cleat the sheet and push the rudder hard over to counter the rotating force of the headsail. The boat will now stay balanced at a close reach angle to the wind on its own.

To start again, the crew releases the headsail and sheets it in on the opposite side. The helm bears away to resume sailing and mainsail is trimmed to suit.

Sail trim

The sails can also have a turning effect on the boat. Bring the boat back into a basic hove-to position, then pull in on the mainsail alone. The boat will turn towards the wind.

Return to the basic hove-to position and then pull in the headsail alone. The boat will turn away from the wind. Keeping the headsail and mainsail sheeted in balance with each other lessens the weight on the helm and the effort needed to steer the boat.

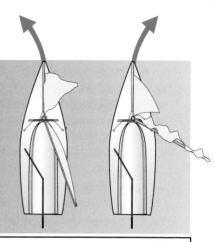

Going about
Turning through 180° from one beam reach angle to the other.

❹ Helm centres rudder on new course. Crew fine-tunes headsail sheet tension. Helm or crew adjusts mainsheet.

❸ As boat passes through the no-go zone, crew loads up headsail sheet on new winch and starts to take up the slack.

❷ Helm and crew look around them to check that it is clear to tack.

❶ Helm calls 'Ready about'. Crew answers 'Ready'.

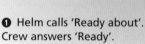

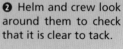

No-go zone

It is not possible to sail directly into the wind, and yachts make headway by making a zigzag tacking course to windward. The angle 45° either side of the wind direction is known as the 'No-go zone. This is when the yacht is pointing directly into wind. The yacht will come to a halt, and, without steerage way, the rudder will have no effect. There is also the danger of the boom thrashing about in the wind and hitting you on the head, so beware. This is the point of sail to be avoided.

Wind

Sail trim

The training run is where the wind is blowing over the quarter, the sails are out and the headsail is empty because it is shielded from the wind by the mainsail.

Practise turning from a beam reach, through a broad reach to the training run and back to sailing close-hauled.

When sailing dead downwind you can set the headsail on the windward side, either by attaching pole between mast and clew of the sail, or by getting a crewmember to stand by the shrouds and hold the headsail sheet out.

Sailing by the lee with the wind crossing the leeward aft quarter should be avoided because the wind can get behind the mainsail, forcing it to swing across in a crash gybe.

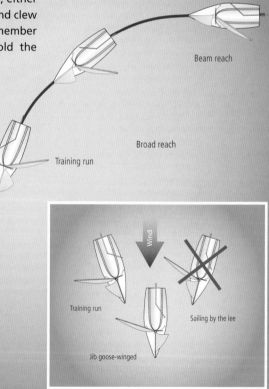

Beam reach

Broad reach

Training run

Close-hauled

Wind

Wind

Training run

Sailing by the lee

Jib goose-winged

Gybing

Gybing takes the back of the boat through the wind. Start from a training run and check to leeward that there are no other boats or hazards in the vicinity.

5 As the mainsail fills on the opposite gybe, the helm sets new course on training run and trims mainsail to suit. Crew adjusts the headsail.

4 Crew trim the headsail sheet on opposite side and let the mainsail sheet run rapidly.

3 As the stern passes through the eye of the wind, helm or crew pulls in the mainsheet to centre the boom. Helm calls 'Gybe ho' and centres the rudder. Crew keep their heads down as the boom swings across and mainsheet is freed to run out rapidly.

Wind

2 Helm calls 'Helm to weather' and pulls the tiller towards him or turns the wheel to bear away.

1 Helm checks that there are no obstructions or boats. Helm or crew hauls in the mainsail close to the centreline of the vessel, and warns the crew with the call 'Ready to gybe'. Crew calls back 'Yes'.

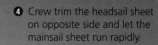

Hand Signals

Hand signals are very useful, because verbal instructions are often carried away on the wind. These are simple ones to remember.

One finger rotating upwards.
Grind in the headsail.

Two fingers rotating upwards.
Grind in the staysail.

One finger rotating downwards.
Ease out the headsail.

Two fingers rotating downwards.
Ease out the staysail.

Clenched fist. STOP!

Crew positions

These are the primary positions on deck. Many cruising yachts are designed to be sailed 'short-handed' with just 2 or 3 active sailors, so some roles such as skipper and navigator, or navigator and cockpit, and mast hand and bowman are doubled up.

H HELM/SKIPPER: Concentrates on steering the yacht and calling when to tack and gybe and changing sails.

N NAVIGATOR: Responsible for communications, navigation and weather information.

G GRINDER: Powers the mainsail, headsail and spinnaker winche.

T TRIMMER: Responsible for trimming headsail and spinnaker sheets.

C COCKPIT HAND: Tails halyards, handles spinnaker pole foreguy and topping lift, reefing lines, headsail roller furling, boom vang and any hydraulics controlled from the cockpit.

M MAST HAND: Responsible for jump-hoisting halyards; sets up inboard end of spinnaker pole, trips spinnaker pole, sets up jockey pole; helps bowman with headsails and spinnakers.

B BOWMAN:
Acts as forward lookout. Responsible for headsail and spinnaker sets and changes; trips spinnaker.

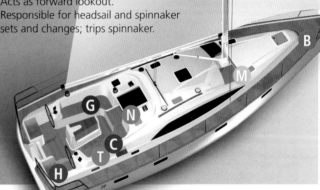

Tacking

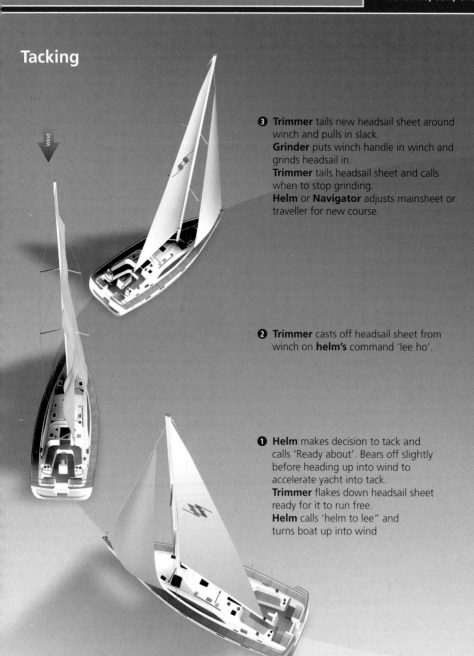

❸ Trimmer tails new headsail sheet around winch and pulls in slack.
Grinder puts winch handle in winch and grinds headsail in.
Trimmer tails headsail sheet and calls when to stop grinding.
Helm or **Navigator** adjusts mainsheet or traveller for new course.

❷ Trimmer casts off headsail sheet from winch on **helm's** command 'lee ho'.

❶ Helm makes decision to tack and calls 'Ready about'. Bears off slightly before heading up into wind to accelerate yacht into tack.
Trimmer flakes down headsail sheet ready for it to run free.
Helm calls 'helm to lee" and turns boat up into wind

Changing sails

Sail changes on a yacht are like gear changes in a car – make them smooth and get back up to speed as quickly as possible. The crew is divided into two groups – the trimmers and the changers. The trimmers concentrate on sail trim all the time, even during evolutions, while the changers execute the evolution as efficiently as possible.

The simplest way to change headsails is to set the yacht on a sea-kindly angle to the sea and wind, release the mainsail sheet to slow the boat down, and then take the headsail down and set the new one. Below is another routine that keeps the yacht sailing and used when club racing. Whichever, the safe way is the quick way – if the change is done properly once, it will be quicker than rushing it twice.

Bald headed headsail change during tack

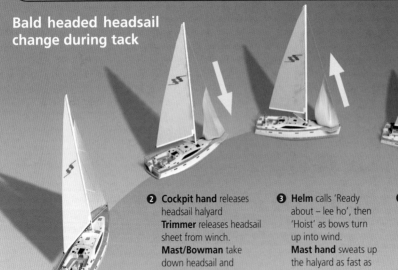

1 **Helm** makes decision to change headsail and calls warning 'Tack headsail change'
Mast/Bowman bring up new headsail, attach tack and secure with sail tie
Cockpit hand flakes down existing headsail halyard ready to run.
Helm calls for headsail drop.

2 **Cockpit hand** releases headsail halyard
Trimmer releases headsail sheet from winch.
Mast/Bowman take down headsail and secure with sail tie.
Bowman hanks new headsail to headstay above hanks of earlier headsail and connects halyard to head. Then calls back to **Cockpit hand** 'Halyard made'.
Mast hand attaches sheets to clew of new headsail.
Trimmer repositions sheet cars to correct position for new sail.

3 **Helm** calls 'Ready about – lee ho', then 'Hoist' as bows turn up into wind.
Mast hand sweats up the halyard as fast as possible at mast.
Cockpit hand tails halyard around winch. When fully hoisted, calls 'Halyard made'.
Trimmer tails new headsail sheet around winch and pulls in slack.

4 **Grinder** puts winch handle in winch and grinds headsail in until **Trimmer** calls 'Stop'
Mast/Bowman unclip old headsail and stow away.
Trimmer leads lazy headsail sheet through correct deck lead.
Crew: Tidy up and move back to standard positions.

Leeward headsail change

① For yachts with twin luff track head foil.
Helm makes decision to change headsail and
calls warning: 'Leeward headsail change'.
Mast/Bowman bring up new headsail
and attach tack and halyard.
Trimmer sets up temporary sheeting system
on headsail already set. Releases old sheet,
connects to clew of new headsail and
changes track car to correct position.

② **Cockpit hand** flakes down existing
headsail halyard ready to run.
Helm/Cockpit hand gives order to hoist.
Bowman feeds luff into headsail hoist.
Mast hand sweats the new
headsail halyard at mast.
Cockpit hand tails halyard around winch.

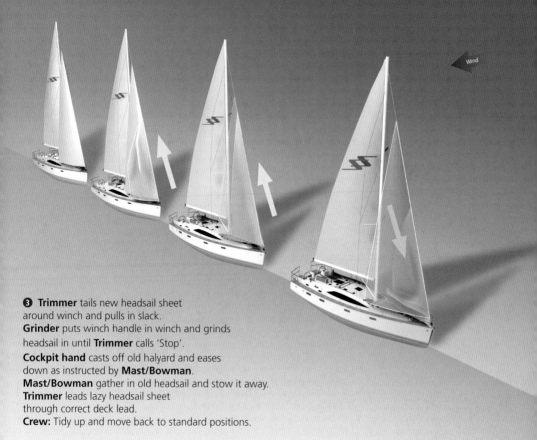

③ **Trimmer** tails new headsail sheet
around winch and pulls in slack.
Grinder puts winch handle in winch and grinds
headsail in until **Trimmer** calls 'Stop'.
Cockpit hand casts off old halyard and eases
down as instructed by **Mast/Bowman**.
Mast/Bowman gather in old headsail and stow it away.
Trimmer leads lazy headsail sheet
through correct deck lead.
Crew: Tidy up and move back to standard positions.

Spinnaker setting

Layout with spinnaker ready to hoist.

1. Sheet
2. Lazy guy
3. Lazy sheet
4. Guy (after guy)
5. Spinnaker (in sail bag on deck)
6. Guy and lazy sheet attached to spinnaker tack
7. Sheet and lazy guy attached to spinnaker clew
8. Spinnaker halyard
9. Lazy sheet led over pole
10. Pole topping lift
11. Pole downhaul (foreguy)

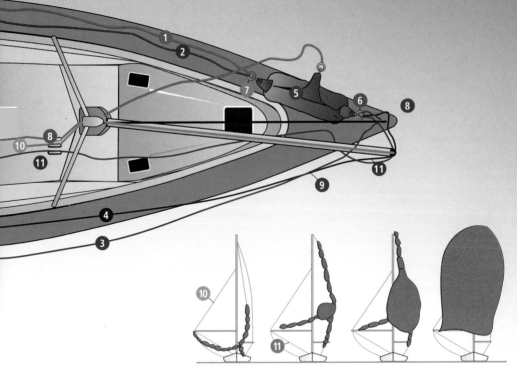

Spinnaker with rubber bands or wool stops to keep the sail from setting prematurely during hoist.

Spinnaker set

❶ Mast/Bowman set up spinnaker pole. **Cockpit hand** sets pole topping lift and downhaul. **Trimmer** sets guy to match wind angle **Helm/Navigator** calls 'Hoist spinnaker'.

❷ Helm makes decision to set spinnaker and calls 'Up Spinnaker'. **Mast/Bowman** bring up spinnaker bag, tie down to deck with sail tie and connect . **Cockpit hand** prepares spinnaker halyard on winch.

❸ Mast hand sweats up the spinnaker halyard. **Cockpit hand** tails halyard and calls 'Halyard made' when fully hoisted. **Trimmer** pulls in spinnaker sheet with **Grinder** winding in on winch.

❹ Cockpit hand releases headsail sheet and furls headsail or flakes down headsail halyard ready to run if sail is coming down. **Mast/Bowman** gather in headsail and tie down on deck. **Cockpit hand** slackens backstay adjustor. **Crew:** Tidy up.

Spinnaker leeward take down

❶ Helm makes decision to take down spinnaker and set headsail. Calls 'Spinnaker leeward takedown – up headsail'. **Cockpit hand** flakes down spinnaker halyard ready to run and prepares to hoist or unfurl headsail. **Mast/Bowman** release sail ties around headsail ready to hoist.

❷ Helm calls 'Drop spinnaker'. **Cockpit hand** casts off spinnaker halyard and **Bowman** releases outboard end of pole. **Trimmer** gathers in lazy (leeward) spinnaker guy. **Helm** starts heading up towards the wind in a controlled manner. **Trimmer** pulls in spinnaker on the lazy guy under the boom and into the cockpit. **Grinder** eases spinnaker guy and sheet. **Cockpit/Mast hand** gather spinnaker in under boom and pass down hatch for repacking.

❸ Mast hand sweats up headsail halyard and **Cockpit hand** tails halyard and calls 'Halyard made' when fully hoisted. **Trimmer** tails headsail sheet and pulls in slack. **Grinder** winds in headsail sheet until **Trimmer** calls 'Stop'

❹ Trimmer/Grinder adjust headsail ltrim for new course. **Cockpit hand** adjusts mainsheet for new course and retensions backstay adjustor. **Bowman** stows spinnaker pole and clears foredeck ready to tack. **Crew:** Tidy up

End-for-end pole gybe

Standard gybing system for open keelboats and small yachts with central pole uphaul and downhaul lines connected centrally to pole.

❶ **Helm** makes decision to gybe and calls warning: 'Prepare spinnaker gybe'. **Navigator/Cockpit hand** pulls mainsail in to centreline. **Trimmer** squares spinnaker aft as **Helm** bears off downwind.

❷ **Bowman** trips spinnaker pole from mast and connects this end to new clew. **Trimmer** keeps spinnaker flying by adjusting sheet and guy simultaneously.

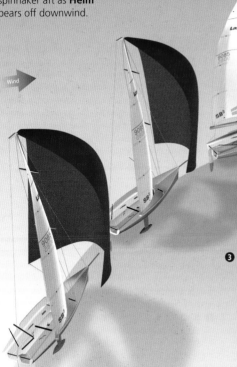

❸ **Helm** calls 'Gybe -ho', turns stern through wind. **Navigator** controls mainsail sheet. **Bowman** trips old spinnaker clew and connects pole end to mast.

❹ **Cockpit hand** adjusts spinnaker pole topping lift. **Trimmer** cleats off spinnaker guy and trims new spinnaker sheet. **Crew:** Tidy up and move back to standard positions.

Dip pole gybe

Standard gybing system for yachts with a single spinnaker pole

❶ **Helm** makes decision to gybe and calls warning: 'Prepare spinnaker gybe'.
Navigator/Cockpit hand pulls mainsail in to centreline.
Trimmer squares spinnaker aft as **Helm** bears off downwind.

❷ **Bowman** trips spinnaker pole from sail.
Trimmer keeps spinnaker flying by adjusting sheet and guy simultaneously.
Cockpit hand lowers spinnaker pole topping lift and takes slack out of foreguy.
Mast hand swings spinnaker pole forward (may have to hoist the pole up the mast to get it inside the forestay).

❸ **Cockpit hand** hoists spinnaker pole topping lift.
Trimmer/Grinder cleat off spinnaker guy and trim new spinnaker sheet.
Helm sets new course and trims mainsail to suit.
Crew: Tidy up

❹ **Bowman** attaches lazy guy to pole end and pushes pole out to new weather side.
Helm calls 'Gybe ho', and turns stern through wind. **Navigator/Cockpit hand** releases mainsheet. **Trimmer** eases foreguy for new course.

Cruising chute (MPS) setting

This sail sets like a loose luffed headsail and is often supplied with a sock or 'snuffer'. If not, then stop the sail with rubber bands or wool prior to hoisting.

❶ **Helm** makes decision to set MPS and calls 'Up cruising chute'. **Mast/Bowman** bring up spinnaker bag and tie down to deck with sail tie. Connect halyard, sheets and tack line.
Cockpit hand prepares spinnaker halyard on winch.

❷ **Helm** calls 'Hoist chute'.
Mast hand jump hoists spinnaker halyard.
Cockpit hand tails halyard and calls 'Halyard made' when fully hoisted.

❹ **Mast hand** hoists 'snuffer' to top of mast.
Trimmer/ Grinder pull in spinnaker sheet with **Grinder** winching until **Trimmer** calls 'stop'.
Bowman checks the tack line for chafe around pulpits, forestay fittings or anchor rollers.
Crew: Tidy up.

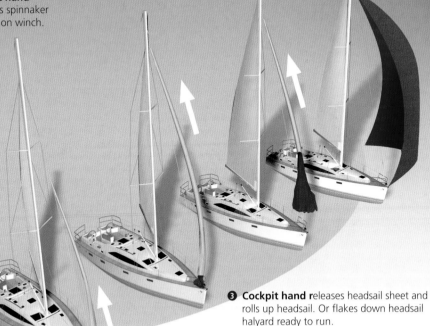

❸ **Cockpit hand** releases headsail sheet and rolls up headsail. Or flakes down headsail halyard ready to run.
Mast/Bowman gather in headsail and tie down on deck.
Navigator slackens backstay adjustor.

Cruising chute – take down

❶ Helm makes decision to take down chute and set headsail.
Calls 'Chute leeward takedown – up headsail'. **Cockpit hand** flakes down spinnaker halyard ready to run and unfurls headsail. Or, **Mast/Bowman** release sail ties around headsail ready to hoist. **Mast hand** sweats up the headsail halyard and **Cockpit hand** tails halyard and calls 'Halyard made' when fully hoisted. **Trimmer** tails headsail sheet and pulls in slack, then releases spinnaker sheet.

❷ Bowman pulls snuffer down from masthead to envelop chute, then calls 'drop chute'.

❸ Grinder winds in headsail sheet until **Trimmer** calls 'Stop'. **Navigator** adjusts mainsheet for new course and retensions backstay adjustor. **Crew:** Tidy up.

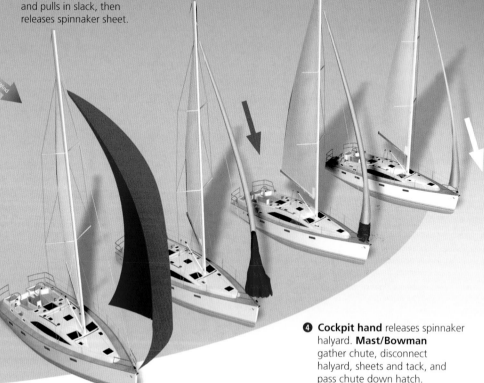

❹ Cockpit hand releases spinnaker halyard. **Mast/Bowman** gather chute, disconnect halyard, sheets and tack, and pass chute down hatch.

Cruising chute – gybe

Standard gybing technique – same as gybing a headsail. If chute is set on a furler, consider furling MPS and unfurling it again after gybing the mainsail.

❶ Helm makes decision to gybe and calls warning 'Prepare to gybe'. **Helm/Navigator** pull mainsail in to centreline. **Trimmer** eases chute as **Helm** bears off downwind.

❷ Helm calls 'Gybe ho', turns stern through wind and releases mainsail sheet. **Trimmer** releases chute sheet.

❸ Trimmer loads new sheet on winch and takes up slack. **Grinder** winches in sheet until **Trimmer** calls 'Stop'. **Crew:** Tidy up.

Tides and weather

To start with, the outside elements of wind and tides can seem complex, but the telltale signs are all easy to read – once you know what to look for.

As UKSA senior instructor Richard Baggett likes to tell his students, 'God gave you ears … to feel which way the wind is coming from. They are the best wind antennae you have, so use them!'

The first rule before going sailing is to check the local weather forecast and tides, which are readily available from the web, weather channels, harbour offices, and even SMS text to your mobile/cell phone.

The second rule is to keep a weather eye out, looking for changes in wind strength or direction by monitoring flags, smoke stacks and other boats around you. The Mark 1 eyeball is an excellent forecasting tool if used regularly.

When the winds are offshore, the seas can be deceptively calm close inshore and require forethought when you return because they will involve beating into wind when heading back. Onshore winds can make it difficult to leave harbour, but once out beyond the influence of land, the waves will invariably lessen, and the wind direction will also make it much easier to return to port later.

Tidal height and flow

Over approximately six and a half hours the height of tide rises to high water, and then over approximately the next six and a half hours falls to low water. This happens with monotonous regularity and is predicted to the minute by tide tables which can be obtained from nautical almanacs, sailing clubs, harbour masters, and directly from the Web. Tides are caused by the interaction between the Sun, the Moon and the Earth. When the three bodies line up (with the new moon – Fig 1, or the full moon – Fig 2) the Sun's and the Moon's gravity directly add to each other, and this causes spring tides, where the high water levels are relatively high, and the low water levels are relatively low. Where the Sun and the Moon

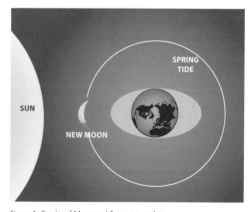

Figure 1: Gravity of Moon and Sun act together

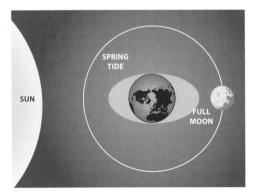

Figure 2: Gravity of Moon and Sun act together

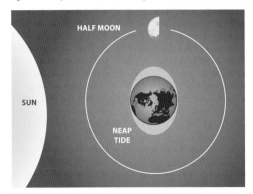

Figure 3: Gravity of Moon and Sun act against each other

are at right angles relative to the Earth (half moon – Fig 3) their respective gravitational pulls are at right angles and therefore not directly adding to each other. This causes neap tides (Fig 5), where the high waters heights are not as high as at springs, and the low water mark is not as low as at springs.

Apart from the obvious point that the height of tide decides which rocks present a danger, the range of tide (the difference in height between high water and low water on a particular day) has a direct bearing on the rate of tidal flow. The time period of the tide is constant, so spring tides have faster rates than neap tides, because they have the same six and a half hours to move a greater volume of water along the coast. Logically, the tide would flood in to high water, and then immediately turn and ebb towards low water. In practice, however, the turn of tidal flow can occur up to two hours before the relevant high or low water. This information can be obtained from tidal stream atlases, local sailors, sailing clubs and harbour masters.

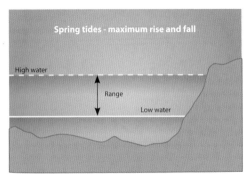

Figure 4

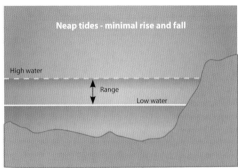

Figure 5

The combination of wind and tide

Tidal rates can vary greatly – 2 knots is fairly average in some locations, and in narrow harbour entrances or gaps between islands it can reach 5 or 6 knots on a regular basis. This has a direct effect on where the journey goes and the sea state during it.

The sea state is generated mostly by the effect of the surface wind on the water. If there is wind with tide (Fig 6), then the sea state will be relatively smooth, and not so choppy. In wind over tide (Fig 7) scenarios this can be quite different, with the waves much shorter and steeper, with a greater risk of flying spray.

If strong winds are forecast, it is important to know when the tide is flooding and ebbing, as that directly affects when the sea state goes from 'Wheeee!' to 'Heeelp!'.

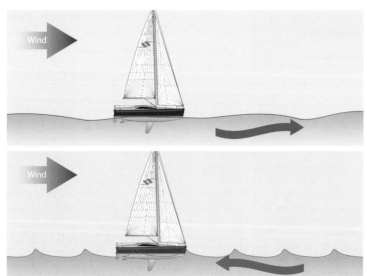

Figure 6. Wind with tide.

Figure 7. Wind over tide.

Perfect sailing conditions

A UKSA offshore training crew being treated to perfect sailing conditions in the Solent, UK. Here, the sun and the onshore component of the prevailing winds help to deliver a healthy sea breeze.

Clouds – what are they and what do they mean?

As air passes over water moisture will be picked up by the air and carried in suspension. The amount of water carried and picked up depends to a large extent on the temperature of the air and the temperature of the water over which it flows. For many reasons this air may then rise or be cooled (or both) and moisture will come out of suspension in the form of water vapour, which is seen as clouds. The type of cloud formed depends on what is happening to the air from which it comes, so the clouds are a good indicator of what the weather is, or is about to be, doing.

There are four main categories of clouds:

Cirrus – a tuft or filament

Cumulus – the classic fluffy cloud

Stratus – layered cloud

Nimbus – rain-bearing cloud (usually a darker more ominous grey)

There are many individual cloud types, the most common are as follows.

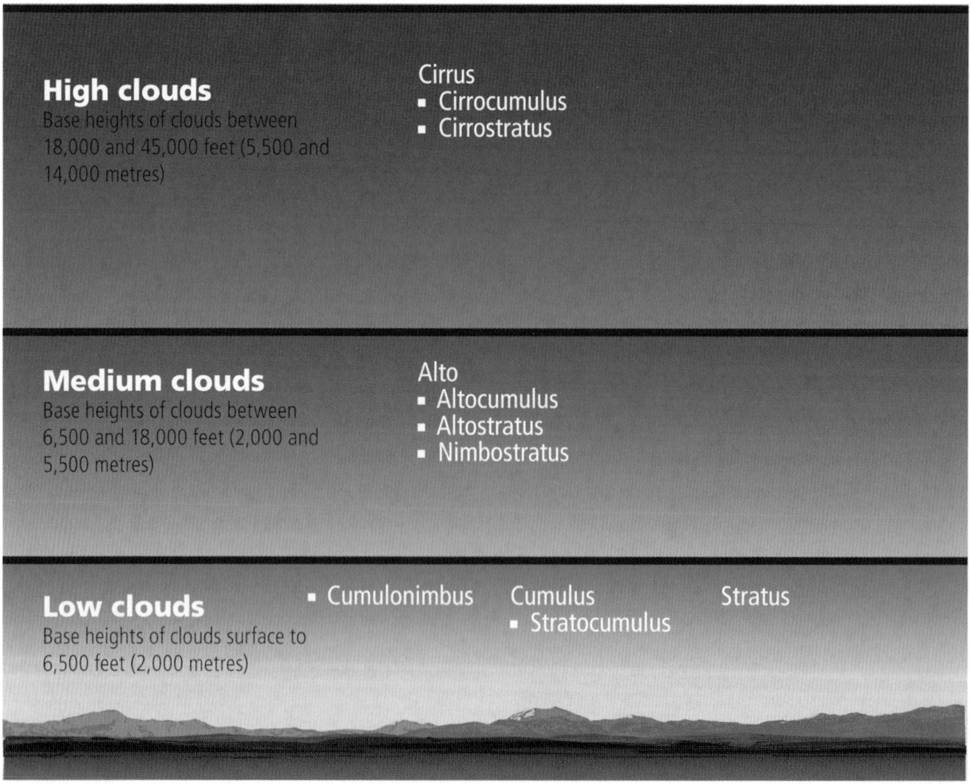

High clouds
Base heights of clouds between 18,000 and 45,000 feet (5,500 and 14,000 metres)

Cirrus
- Cirrocumulus
- Cirrostratus

Medium clouds
Base heights of clouds between 6,500 and 18,000 feet (2,000 and 5,500 metres)

Alto
- Altocumulus
- Altostratus
- Nimbostratus

Low clouds
Base heights of clouds surface to 6,500 feet (2,000 metres)

- Cumulonimbus Cumulus Stratus
  - Stratocumulus

Cirrus: long feathery filaments of ice crystals often associated with tufts known as 'mares' tails'. These are typically associated with the approach of a frontal system, meaning that changeable weather is on the way in the next 24 hours.

Cirrocumulus: known as a 'mackerel sky' they are composed of collections of high altitude ice crystals and look like rippled sand on a beach. These are typically associated with the approach of a frontal system.

Cirrostratus: a more continuous high level layer of ice crystals, again associated with an approaching frontal system. This cloud may give rise to a halo around the sun and the moon.

Altocumulus: thin, broken up fluffy clouds, they are the next indicator after the cirrus clouds that a frontal system, and therefore rain, is on the way in the next 12 hours or so.

Altostratus: a thin, reasonably consistent layer of cloud through which the sun will shine weakly. There will be patches of darker grey in it, and this is an imminent precursor to rain and the arrival of a front.

Nimbostratus: a darker, heavier version of stratus clouds, with identifiable features that can hang off the base of the main formation almost like large sacks of rain waiting to fall. Any precipitation is likely to be heavy, with some unpredictable wind shifts and gusts on the edges of these showers.

Stratus: a most depressing low, uniform grey layer of cloud with few identifiable features. There will be scattered drizzle and light rain under these, and they generally occur at the end of fronts or in the warm sector of a frontal system.

Cumulus: individual white or light grey fluffy clouds, often seen along coastlines in the afternoon as a result of warm air rising as the day heats up or in the relatively dry air following the passing of a frontal system. They are a good indicator of fair weather.

Stratocumulus: layered cumulus clouds, generally white or light grey in patches. These are not threatening, and generally the worst that will happen is the occasional shower.

Cumulonimbus: these clouds are typically associated with cold fronts, often forming line squalls just in front of them. They are typically low based but can reach up as high as 40,000 feet (12,000 meters), and are very energetic, dark and forbidding formations, generating rain, hail, thunder and lightning, as well as unpredictable strong squalls around their edges and underneath them. They can be embedded in layers of stratocumulus and can be spotted by their extremely dark bases and characteristic anvil top.

Red sky at night, sailor's delight: this saying is often true – if a frontal system has passed over from west to east, as is generally the case, then the setting sun in the west will light up the clouds at the back of the system as it takes the rain away with it to the east.

Red sky in the morning, sailor's warning: as the rising sun in the east lights up approaching clouds in the west, the frontal system is on the way.

Beaufort Wind Scale

Force	Speed	Description	Observations	Sail choice
0	0–1 knots	Calm	Sea like a mirror. Smoke rises vertically.	Full sail – crew to leeward.
1	1–3 knots	Light air	Ripples have appearance of scales on water. Smoke drift and flags indicate direction.	Full sail
2	4–6 knots	Light breeze	Small wavelets with glassy crests. Wind can be felt on the face. Flags and wind vanes also indicate direction.	Full sail
3	7–10 knots	Gentle breeze	Large wavelets. Crests begin to break producing scattered white horses. Leaves and branches begin to move. Ideal conditions to learn to sail.	1st reef in mainsail
4	11–16 knots	Moderate breeze	Small waves, becoming larger; frequent white horses. Keelboats require more work to keep balanced.	2nd reef in mainsail. Headsail $^1/_3$ furled
5	17–21 knots	Fresh winds	Moderate waves, take a more pronounced form with regular white horses formed with spray. Chance of broaching. Small trees sway in wind and flags flying horizontally.	2nd reef in mainsail. Headsail ½ furled
6	22–27 knots	Strong winds	Large waves with white foam crests and spray are extensive. Limit of safety for small keelboats. Large trees sway and wind whistles.	3rd reef in mainsail. Headsail $^2/_3$ furled or storm headsail set
7	28–33 knots	Near gale	Sea heaps up and white foam from breaking waves begins to be blown in streaks along the direction of the wind.	3rd reef in mainsail or storm trisail with storm headsail
8	34–40 knots	Gale	Moderately high waves of greater length; edges of crests begin to break into spindrift. The foam is blown in well-marked streaks along the direction of the wind.	Head for port!

Frontal systems and weather maps

Most weather is caused by the passage of frontal systems, or depressions, or low pressure systems over the continent. A basic understanding of these and regular looks at the associated synoptic chart (the weather map) will soon allow a reasonable level of forecasting ability to be attained.

The basic source of weather is the interaction between different air masses. Broadly speaking there are four types of air mass:

Polar air masses: cold and dry air from the polar regions

Tropical air masses: warm, wet air from the tropical ocean areas

Maritime air masses: relatively wet air coming from nontropical ocean areas

Continental air masses: relatively dry air coming from large land masses

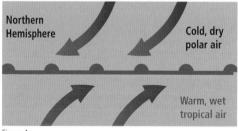

Figure 1a

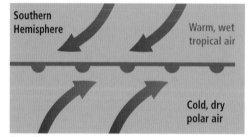

Figure 1b

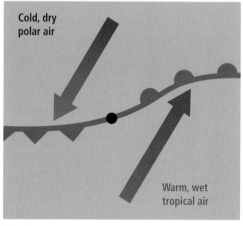

Figure 2

The frontal systems that cause most European weather are caused by the interaction of cold dry polar air coming from the Arctic and the warm wet air coming from the Atlantic.

An eddy forms (just like those seen in water running by a pontoon), and the system may start to rotate (anticlockwise in the Northern Hemisphere (Figure 1a), clockwise in the Southern (Figure 1b).

This is where two major features are formed – the warm and cold fronts. These are quite simply the front of the relatively warm and wet and relatively cold and dry air masses (Figure 2). A domestic example is the bathroom in the morning. Hot, moisture-laden air meets a cold, dry mirror, and condensation immediately forms. Warm and cold fronts are much larger versions of that, but are fundamentally down to the meeting of two different air masses. The section of air between the two fronts is the relatively warm and wet air mass, known as the warm sector.

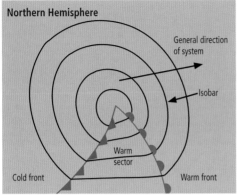

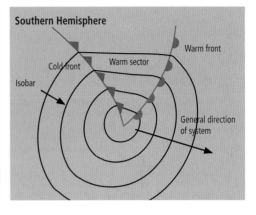

Figure 3

With the frontal system fully developed and usually moving to the north-east or east, there is a complete circulation around the centre of the low, just as in little whirlpools on the edge of a fast flowing stream. This can be seen in terms of a pressure map, otherwise known as a synoptic chart (Figure 3).

Here, the warm and cold fronts are represented, and the shape of the system as a whole is shown by the isobars, or lines of equal pressure. These isobars are the first

forecasting tool, as the wind direction is generally about 10 to 15° off the line of the isobar, offset inwards towards the centre of the low. Wind strength is directly related to the spacing between the isobars (the pressure gradient Figure 4). The closer the isobars, the more the pressure gradient, and therefore the stronger the wind. Once the wind direction and strength have been looked at, the weather is next. This is driven by what is happening in the air above the boat.

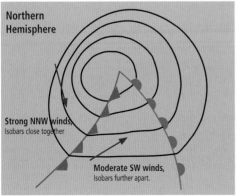

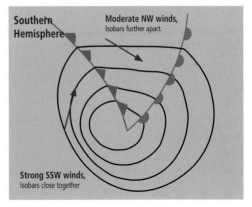

Figure 4

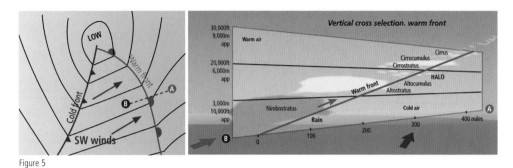

Figure 5

As the front goes over, the rain will reach its maximum, and the visibility will drop. Once the front has passed, the rain will ease up, and the visibility will improve, but not back to how it was before the front, as the warm sector air mass is relatively warm and wet and so will hold more moisture and not be as clear (Figure 5). The cloud cover will be mostly stratus or nimbostratus, and there may be fairly steady rain. The wind will have veered, and will be reasonably constant in strength and direction.

The cold front is a very different animal to the warm front. As the air mass is cold and dry, it cannot climb up and over the warm sector air mass, so all the interaction between the two air masses happens in almost the same vertical plane, potentially allowing the formation of massive cumulonimbus clouds (Figure 6). The conditions under the front are potentially dangerous, with unpredictable squalls coming off the edges of the cumulonimbus clouds, heavy rain or hail and electrical storms all possible. As a result of all this, visibility may be very poor.

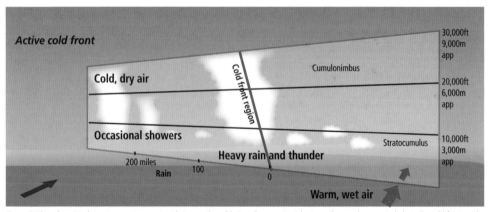

Figure 6 When there is a large temperature contrast between the cold air and warm air, violent weather can be expected along the cold front, with rain squalls and perhaps hail and thunder.

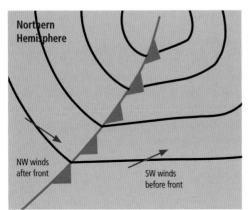

Figure 7a

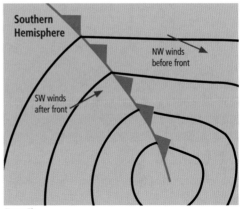

Figure 7b

After the cold front has passed, however, the wind will veer again, the skies will clear almost immediately, and as the air is now part of the cold, dry mass, the visibility will be excellent and there may be some scenic cumulus clouds if any (Figure 7).

As the whole system becomes more mature the cold front will start to catch up with the warm front, very much like a zipper being done up. This forms an occluded front and results in what's left of the warm sector being pushed up above the preceding and following cold air masses which now join up (Figure 8).

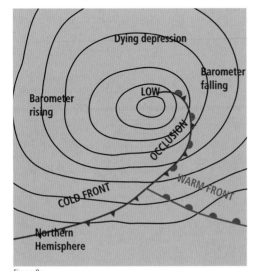

Figure 8a

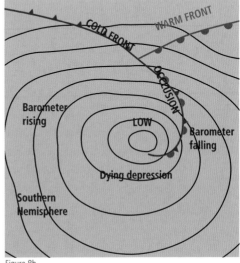

Figure 8b

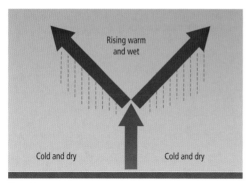

Figure 9

Atlantic or Azores High. They are not as mobile as low pressure systems, and are also generally composed of just one air mass, and so do not have the fronts associated with a low. In the Northern Hemisphere they rotate clockwise (anticlockwise in the Southern Hemisphere) and are represented by isobars as with low pressure systems.

The same rules apply for wind strength and direction as before – the direction of the isobars is broadly speaking the direction of the wind around the high, with the wind offset by 10 to 15 degrees away from the centre of it. The wind strength is governed by the spacing in between the isobars, the pressure gradient.

High pressure systems can bring balmy weather, and in European waters over summer this is often the case, with the centre of a high sitting over northern France bringing light and variable winds to most of the European continent.

However, if a relatively static high acts as a buffer for a strong low (Fig 10), then very large pressure gradients can occur between the

As all this warm wet air is lifted, it cools, causing moisture to come out of the air in the form of a persistent, miserable drizzle and low level cloud. (Figure 9). As this is towards the end of the frontal system's life it's normally not very energetic.

High pressure systems and their interaction with low pressure systems

High pressure systems are generally found over large ocean masses, for example the North

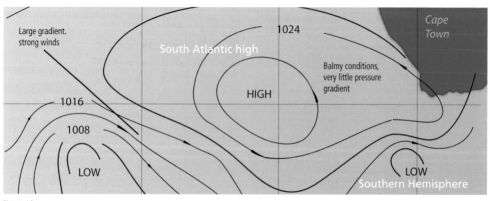

Figure 10

systems, causing very strong winds, as illustrated, for the Southern Hemisphere.

Fog

Fog is basically sea level cloud, and is caused in two ways: radiation or land fog. This occurs either when there is not much gradient wind, there is a change in sea temperature or a drop in wind speed. A high pressure system overhead is an ideal circumstance.

During the day the air will heat up over the shore and over the sea, and moisture will be taken in by the air as it heats up (Figure 11). As soon as the sun goes down, the air will cool and start to release this moisture in the form of fog. It will collect in low lying areas, e.g. harbours and river valleys, and will occasionally spill out up to two or three miles from land. When the sun rises, the air will heat up again, the moisture will go back into suspension, and the fog will clear – this is what is meant by the sun 'burning off' the fog. So, if at breakfast there is no visibility and little wind, then by about 11:00 the fog will have gone and sailing will be possible (depending on the wind).

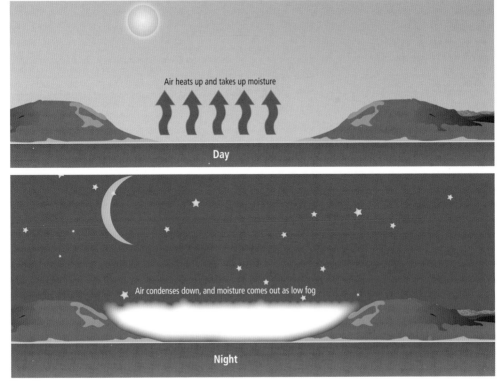

Air heats up and takes up moisture

Day

Air condenses down, and moisture comes out as low fog

Night

Figure 11

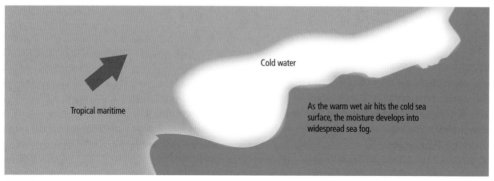

Tropical maritime

Cold water

As the warm wet air hits the cold sea surface, the moisture develops into widespread sea fog.

Figure 12

After the sun goes down, the air cools, releasing moisture, which develops into night fog (Fig 12).

Advection, or sea fog

This is caused by relatively warm wet air blowing over cold water. The cold sea surface cools the surface air, causing the moisture to come out of suspension as fog. This occurs mostly in the spring, when water temperature is coldest after winter and the tropical maritime air masses are being brought in from warmer latitudes (Figure 13).

This fog is more difficult to shift. An increase in wind speed just brings in more moisture, and sea fog can still be there in strong winds. Because new moisture is being brought in constantly, the sun cannot heat up the air sufficiently. The only way sea fog can dissipate is when there is a change in moisture, temperature or wind (Figure 13).

Visibility	
Good	More than 5 miles (9.25km)
Moderate	2-5 miles (3.7-9.25km)
Poor	0.5-2 miles (1-3.7km)
Fog	Less than 0.5mile (1km)

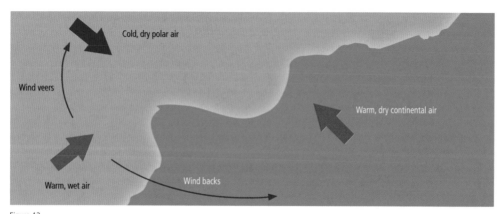

Cold, dry polar air

Wind veers

Warm, dry continental air

Warm, wet air

Wind backs

Figure 13

Weather terms

Barometric tendency – The rise or fall of the barometer at three-hour intervals, giving an early indication to a change in the weather.

Cyclonic – Term often used in shipping forecasts when a low is tracking through a sea area and wind shifts are difficult to predict.

Depressions – Rotating frontal systems.

Front – The front edge of a relatively warm, wet air mass (for a warm front) or a relatively cold, dry air mass (for a cold front).

Gradient wind – The wind caused by pressure difference. Wind flowing from high and low pressure, which is affected by the rotation of the Earth's surface, causing it to blow around high and low pressure systems. The closer the isobars, the stronger the wind.

Gusts – Parcels of fast-moving air sucked down by rising thermal currents, which last for several minutes. Strong gusts occur when the descending upper wind is reinforced by down draughts on the surface generated by heavy rain and thunderstorms.

Line squall – A cold front often marked by a line of low black cloud, which brings with it a sharp rise in wind speed and direction for a short term.

Mistral – Localized strong to gale force wind. This particular wind refers to the predictable slope wind that blows down the Rhône Valley and extends out across the Rhône delta into the Gulf of Lions. Forecasters can usually predict its passage to within minutes. This phenomena occurs in many parts of the world. It is known as the Meltemi in the Aegean Sea, Tramontana or Garigliano on the west coast of Italy and northern Corsica, and the Hamatan off West Africa.

Troughs – Frontal troughs are easily recognizable as a line of changing weather. Non-frontal troughs are harder to pick up, as the air mass does not change discernibly as the front passes through. However, the pressure falls ahead and rises behind and winds back ahead and veer behind. Troughs often follow a cold front and rotate around a depression like the spokes of a wheel.

Veering and backing winds – A veering wind changes direction in a clockwise direction and a backing wind moves anticlockwise.

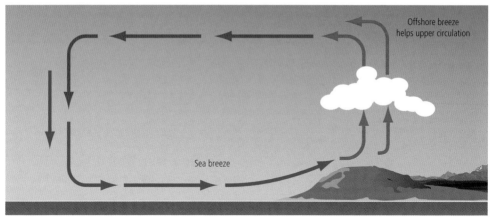

Offshore breeze helps upper circulation

Sea breeze

Figure 14

Sea breezes

Sea breezes are a sailor's lifeline on hot, balmy summer days. They are caused by the difference in warming characteristics between land and sea (Figure 14).

The land will heat up faster than the sea, and so the air above the land will heat up faster than that above the sea. This makes it expand and rise up. As it expands upwards, it also expands outwards, and pushes out to sea. As there is now physically less air over the land and more air over the sea, a localized low pressure is formed over the land, and a localized high pressure is formed over the sea, which causes a sea level breeze– the sea breeze– to blow from the sea towards the shore.

As the afternoon wears on, the continual rising of moisture laden air above the land will cause cumulus clouds to form along the coast. Also, if there is a slight offshore high level wind, this helps the development of the sea breeze.

Wind shadows and funnelling

These two effects are entirely local, and are a function of large obstructions around and through which the wind has to pass.

Any tall object, such as a moored cargo ship or a large headland, will have a wind shadow on its leeward side (Figure15). As an approximate rule of thumb the wind shadow of an obstruction will be approximately six times its height. By looking for ripples on the water it is often possible to see where the wind shadow finishes, and plan the route accordingly.

Tips

❶ Know your limitations.

❷ Always get a forecast for the time you intend to sail plus a bit.

❸ Always tell someone where you are going and when you intend to be back.

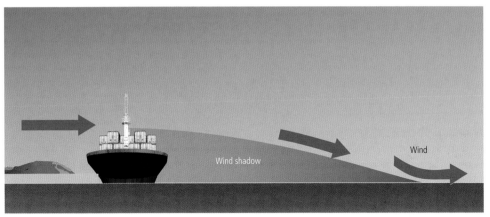

Figure 15

When sailing in estuaries or harbours with tall buildings nearby, there will be alleys between these obstructions where the wind will be funnelled, causing very sudden and local areas of increased and possibly shifted wind (Figure16). Again, by keeping an eye open for the change in surface ripples caused by a change in wind characteristics, some warning can be had. Another sign will be yachts in front of you suddenly heeling heavily while sailing upwind, or broaching out of control when sailing downwind.

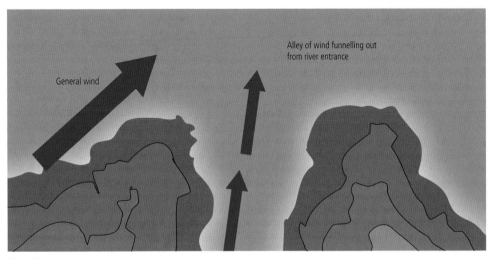

Figure 16

Basics of navigation

Nautical charts – there is no substitute

An acquaintance once boasted to me that he had navigated a powerboat from the Solent to Guernsey using a road atlas. Someone above must have been looking after him, especially in the rock-strewn passages through the Channel Islands because none of those hazards would have been shown. Quite apart from endangering his own life and that of his crew, his insurance would have been invalidated too!

A chart catalogue highlights the coverage of each chart and its number. The UK Hydrographic Office produces standard charts for every part of the world. NOAA's Office of Coastal Survey does the same for the coastal waters of the US and its territories. There are also small-craft charts designed for use on small chart tables, and others available from specialist chart manufacturers. If you are using electronic charts displayed on a plotter or PC, always carry a paper chart as back up – just in case the electronics fail.

Chart projections

Projection is a way to present the globe as a flat chart. A Gnomonic projection is used for ocean charts and shows the world in 3D, while the Mercator projection, which is commonly used for coastal charts, shows the lines of longitude in parallel. Imagine a sheet of paper wrapped around the Earth, touching around the Equator. If you turn on bright light at the centre of the planet, the shadows of the land masses and lines of latitude and longitude will be projected on this paper. This Mercator projection converts the constant bearing lines around the globe into straight lines on the charts. These are known as rhumb lines.

Charts must be kept up to date. Minor corrections will be found in weekly updates published as 'Notices to Mariners' **www.nga.mil** for all US issued charts; **www.nmwebsearch.com** for all UK issued charts. When major corrections are made, publishers will issue a new edition. Electronic charts can be updated online or with a CD ROM. Pilot books and nautical almanacs provide detailed information about ports, including tidal heights, streams, pilotage notes and contact information for marinas and harbour authorities: **www.wileynautical.com** for the Thames, English Channel and adjacent coasts; **http://asa.usno.navy.mil** for an astronomical nautical almanac; **http://aa.usno.navy.mil** for a US nautical almanac.

This gives the most familiar chart, where the latitude scale 'stretches' the further north or south you are from the Equator.

With further manipulation the final projection is as shown on the left.

The two projections (right) are 'cylindrical' projections, as they effectively wrap a cylinder around the globe.

One common 'zenithal' projection is the gnomonic projection shown here, which is used for ocean navigation.

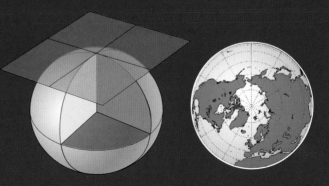

Title information on charts

This is very important, as it defines what units are used for measurement, how you plot positions on the chart and where the actual chart data comes from, as well as important information specific to the charted area.

As an example, let's look at Admiralty Chart 1400, the Outer Approaches to Puerto Cristóbal on the north coast of Panama, printed in 2006.

Depths: These are given in metres. Many charts are still in fathoms and feet, so do check. Charts outside European waters often refer to 'Mean Lower Low Water' (MLLW). This is similar to 'Mean Low Water Springs', and a table is provided on the chart.

Heights: Areas of drying heights, i.e. parts of the seabed that are not always covered by the sea, are marked in green, with the actual drying height above Chart Datum underlined, as shown below.

Other heights, for example the heights of lights and the clearance of bridges and power cables, are specified for each chart. In this case, it is above Mean High Higher Water, on other charts it is Mean High Water Springs, and on charts printed after 2004, it may be Highest Astronomical Tide. This is important to check.

Positions: In this case the chart is a World Geodetic System chart (WGS84), so GPS positions on this datum can be plotted directly onto it. This is not always the case – so do check it.

Navigational marks: IALA B in this case – 'red right return' (See page 141). If the Americas are your first landfall since leaving Europe, this may come as a surprise.

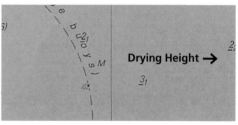

Drying Height →

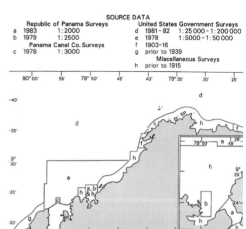

SATELLITE-DERIVED POSITIONS

Positions obtained from satellite navigation systems, such as the Global Positioning System (GPS), are normally referred to the World Geodetic System 1984 Datum. Such positions can be plotted directly on this chart.

POSITIONS: CHARTS 2417,2145

Positions on larger scale chart 2417 and smaller scale chart 2145 differ from those on this chart by varying amounts. Accordingly, positions should be transferred by bearing and distance from common charted objects and not by latitude and longitude.

EXPLOSIVES ANCHORAGE
(9°24′3N, 79°56′8W)

Ships carrying dangerous cargoes are t await instructions from the Port Captai before anchoring.

Other information: On each chart there will be local information, for example, the explosives anchorage detailed here. If you have not been to this area before it is important to read this thoroughly.

Projection: With a Mercator chart you can measure bearings directly.

Sources: Very important. Not all the survey data is recent, as shown above. Here, the most recent data is from 1983 with some areas not surveyed since 1915, and if the bottom is coral or sand, as opposed to rock, it may have changed dramatically.

Chart corrections

Paper charts must be kept up-to-date with changes published in the weekly *Notices to Mariners* (see page 130). Corrections applied to charts should be made in magenta pen and then added to the bottom left corner of the chart. You should also carry an inventory of the charts on board and catalogue the corrections that have been applied.

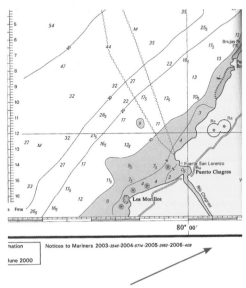

Add new chart corrections in magenta pen here and note the year

Latitude and longitude

All meridians of longitude are great circles, meaning they cut the earth exactly in half between the Poles. Meridians of longitude are marked 180° West and 180° East from the Greenwich Meridian, now known as Universal Time Coefficient (UTC), due to the fact that the French pay for the nuclear clocks from which time is measured. Latitude is measured from the Equator, 90° North and 90° South; the Equator is the only great circle in the parallels of latitude.

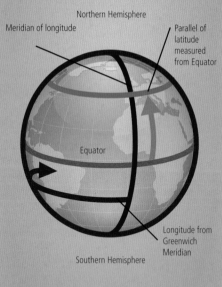

Northern Hemisphere

Meridian of longitude

Parallel of latitude measured from Equator

Equator

Longitude from Greenwich Meridian

Southern Hemisphere

1 degree of latitude = 60 minutes (') of arc
1 degree of latitude = 60 nautical miles
1' of latitude = 1 nautical mile (average)
1 nautical mile = 1852 metres
1' of latitude = 10 cables
1 cable = 180m

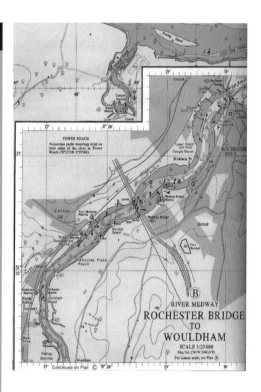

Reading positions

The latitude comes from the vertical axis, i.e. north/south, and longitude comes from the horizontal axis, i.e. east/west, shown above.

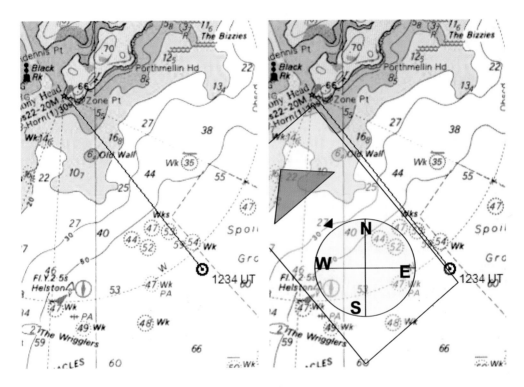

Measuring a course on a chart

This is a fundamental chart function, and starts by drawing a line from the place where you want to take the bearing toward the place you want to take the bearing to.

In this example, if you've put a fix on the chart at 1234UT (the log reading is in brackets) and want to find the bearing of St Anthony Head lighthouse in order to be able to identify it on the shore, draw a line from your position to the lighthouse.

Then put your plotter on the chart parallel to the line you've drawn with the big arrow on the main part of the plotter pointing towards

the lighthouse, i.e. along the bearing. Line up the circular bearing wheel at the centre of the plotter so that the N/S line on that wheel lines up with a convenient N/S line on the chart, and read off the bearing – in this case 322° (true).

Always ask yourself if this makes sense – at 0230 it can be easy to get things 180° out, but by saying '322° – that's roughly NW – that looks right, I know Falmouth's roughly that way' you can save yourself a lot of mistakes. Had you got it 180° out, it would have been '142° – that's roughly SE – hang on – that's where France is!'.

Measuring distances

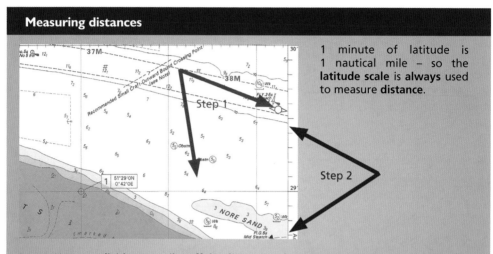

1 minute of latitude is 1 nautical mile – so the **latitude scale** is **always** used to measure **distance**.

Step 1: Use your dividers to scribe off the distance to be measured, in this case between the 5.5m depth Obstruction & the Reach No 1 buoy.

Step 2: Keeping the dividers at the same width (you need a set which is stiff enough to hold a setting, but not so stiff you can't move them), move them to the latitude scale, and measure the distance – in this case 0.55 nautical miles.

Be careful to measure distances at roughly the same latitude at which you first measure them – due to the Mercator projection of a 3D globe onto a 2D chart, the scale will change as the latitude changes. Try it on a chart that covers 50 miles or more.

Electronic navigation techniques

Satellite navigation systems are now widely available, and standard on most yachts. The most common system is the Global Positioning System (GPS), which allows you to navigate to an accuracy of a few tens of metres anywhere in the world.

Each individual set will have its own specific operating instructions, and this section deals with how you use the data from the instrument, not on the specific operating methods.

VERY IMPORTANT

It is **vital** that the datum used by the chart you are working on is the same as the datum used by your GPS set. (See page 148). If these are not the same, significant and dangerous navigational errors can occur. Similarly, some of the most beautiful parts of the world (Indian Ocean, Caribbean and South Pacific islands) have significant chart datum differences. **Always back up close quarters GPS with visual and radar fixes.**

Basic GPS outputs and their derivatives

GPS sets directly measure position and the way that position changes. The basic outputs are:

Position: Latitude and longitude

SOG: Speed over ground

COG: Course over ground

You can input waypoints to the GPS set, and set it to navigate between them as a route. Derived from this are:

DTG: Distance to go to next waypoint or end of route.

BTW: Bearing to next waypoint. This can be set to degrees True or Magnetic.

TTG: Time to go to next waypoint or end of route. This is usually derived from DTG and VMG, and is an instantaneous reading, not an average one.

XTE: Cross track error with respect to the ideal

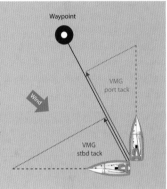

Waypoint

VMG: Velocity made good towards the next waypoint. The diagram above shows that only a proportion of the vessel's velocity is actually going directly for the waypoint. In this case, the wind is coming from the port side of the waypoint so the port tack gets you towards the waypoint far quicker. It has a better VMG and is the **making tack**. This gets looked at constantly while racing, and for cruising it is a useful indicator of the efficiency of your course when you have a restaurant booking waiting for you.

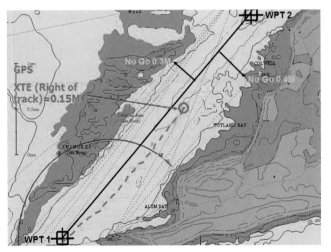

track between waypoints. On the screen below, the XTE is being monitored either side of the ideal track.

Using GPS data efficiently

Position fixing can be done in several ways. There is obviously the direct transposition of latitude and longitude onto the chart, but there are several faster ways of doing it.

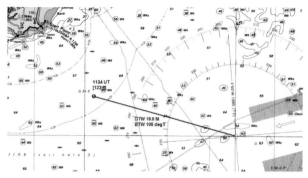

Distance and bearing to waypoint

The centre of the nearest compass rose is ideal for this. By plotting the bearing and distance to waypoint you can get a fix with only one plotter line – very efficient and quick. The waypoint doesn't have to be one you are actually going to, but one that your GPS is programmed to give data relative to.

Electronic charts

The logical step from using your GPS data on a paper chart is to feed it directly into an electronic chart, and get a continuous up-to-date plot of where you are. This is really convenient, but it is vital to keep a regular log entry going, because if the technology fails then you need to be able to move back to paper from your last known point.

There are two types of electronic charts – raster and vector charts.

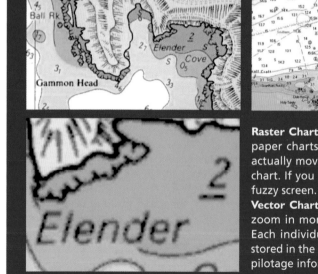

Raster Charts are scanned versions of the paper charts, and when you zoom in you actually move from chart to more detailed chart. If you zoom in too far you just get a fuzzy screen.

Vector Charts have layered data – as you zoom in more and more data is revealed. Each individual feature has data about it stored in the chart, giving you a lot of useful pilotage information.

Buoys, lights and how to use them

Light characteristics

Lighthouses are generally the most complex of these. A lighthouse could have the characteristic:

> **Oc.WR.15s.23m.22-20M**
> **Horn(1)30s**

This means it is **Oc**culting, (a rhythmic light where the duration of light in each period is longer than the duration of darkness) has **W**hite & **R**ed sectors, repeating every **15s**, the main lamp is **23m** above Mean High Water Springs (MHWS), the White is visible for **22** nautical miles, the Red **20**. In restricted visibility, it will sound a **horn** -once every **30s**.

Isolated danger marks

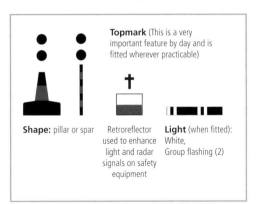

Topmark (This is a very important feature by day and is fitted wherever practicable)

Shape: pillar or spar

Retroreflector used to enhance light and radar signals on safety equipment

Light (when fitted): White, Group flashing (2)

Safe water marks

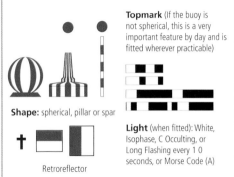

Topmark (If the buoy is not spherical, this is a very important feature by day and is fitted wherever practicable)

Shape: spherical, pillar or spar

Retroreflector

Light (when fitted): White, Isophase, C Occulting, or Long Flashing every 1 0 seconds, or Morse Code (A)

Special marks

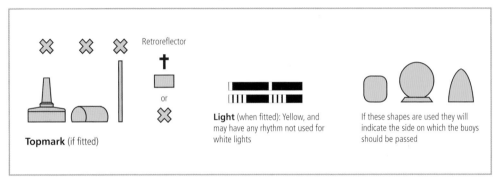

Retroreflector

or

Topmark (if fitted)

Light (when fitted): Yellow, and may have any rhythm not used for white lights

If these shapes are used they will indicate the side on which the buoys should be passed

Light Characters Light Characters on Light Buoys ---> IQ			
Abbreviation		Class of Light	Illustration Period shown
International	National		
		Fixed	
Occulting (total duration of light longer than total duration of darkness)			
Oc	Occ	Single-occulting	
Oc(2)	GpOcc(2)	Group-occulting	
Oc(2+3)	GpOcc(2+3)	Composite group-occulting	
Isophase (duration of light and darkness equal)			
Iso	Isophase		
Flashing (total duration of light shorter than total duration of darkness)			
Fl		Single-flashing	
Fl(3)	GpFl(3)	Group-flashing	
Fl(2+1)	GpFl(2+1)	Composite group-flashing	
L Fl		Long-flashing	
Quick (repetition rate of 50 to 79 – usually either 50 or 60 flashes per minute)			
Q	QkFl	Continuous quick	
Q(3)	QkFl(3)	Group quick	
IQ	IntQkFl	Interrupted quick	
Very quick (repetition rate of 80 to 159 – usually either 100 or 120 flashes per minute)			
VQ	VQkFl	Continuous very quick	
VQ(3)	VQkFl(3)	Group very quick	
IVQ	IntVkFl	Interrupted very quick	
Ultra quick (repetition rate of 160 or more – usually 240 to 300 flashes per minute)			
UQ		Continuous ultra quick	
IUQ		Group ultra quick	
Mo(K)		Morse Code	
FFl		Fixed and flashing	
Al.WR	Alt.Wr	Alternating	

Region A

This diagram is schematic and in the case of pillar buoys in particular, their features will vary with the individual design of the buoys in use.

PORT HAND
Colour: Red.
Shape: Can, pillar or spar.
Topmark (when fitted):
Single red can.
Retroreflector: Red band or square.

PORT HAND
Colour: Red.
Shape: Can, pillar or spar.
Topmark (when fitted):
Single red can.
Retroreflector: Red band or square.

Direction of buoyage

LIGHTS, when fitted, may have any rhythm other than composite group flashing (2+ l) used on modified lateral marks indicating a preferred channel. Examples are:

O.R	Continuous-quick light	O.G
Fl.R	Single-flashing light	Fl.G
LFl.R	Long-flashing light	LFl.G
Fl(2)R	Group-flashing light	Fl(2)G

The lateral colours of red or green are frequently used for minor shore lights, such as those marking pier heads and the extremities of jetties.

Preferred channel to starboard
Colour: Red with one broad green band.
Shape: Can, pillar or spar.
Topmark (when fitted):
Single red can.
Retroreflector:
Red band or square.

Preferred channel to port
Colour: Green with one broad red band.
Shape: Conical, pillar or spar.
Topmark (when fitted): Single green cone point upward.
Retroreflector:
Green band or triangle.

Direction of buoyage

Fl(2+1)R   Composite group flashing (2+ l) light   Fl(2+ 1)G

Where port or starboard marks do not rely on can or conical buoy shapes for identification, they carry the appropriate topmark where practicable or lettered, the numbering or lettering follows the conventional direction of buoyage e. Special marks, with can and conical shapes but painted yellow, may be used in conjunction with the standard lateral marks for special types of channel.

Region B

This diagram is schematic and in the case of pillar buoys in particular, their features will vary with the individual design of the buoys in use.

PORT HAND
Colour: Red.
Shape: Can, pillar or spar.
Topmark (when fitted):
Single red can.
Retroreflector: Red band or square.

PORT HAND
Colour: Red.
Shape: Can, pillar or spar.
Topmark (when fitted):
Single red can.
Retroreflector: Red band or square.

Direction of buoyage

LIGHTS, when fitted, may have any rhythm other than composite group flashing (2+ l) used on modified Lateral marks indicating a preferred channel. Examples are:

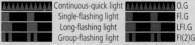

O.R	Continuous-quick light	O.G
Fl.R	Single-flashing light	Fl.G
LFl.R	Long-flashing light	LFl.G
Fl(2)R	Group-flashing light	Fl(2)G

The lateral colours of red or green are frequently used for minor shore lights, such as those marking pier heads and the extremities of jetties.

Preferred channel to starboard
Colour: Red with one broad green band.
Shape: Can, pillar or spar.
Topmark (when fitted):
Single red can.
Retroreflector:
Red band or square.

Preferred channel to port
Colour: Green with one broad red band.
Shape: Conical, pillar or spar.
Topmark (when fitted): Single green cone, point upward.
Retroreflector: Green band or triangle.

Direction of buoyage

Fl(2+1)R   Composite group flashing (2+ l) light   Fl(2+ 1)G

Where port or starboard marks do not rely on can or conical buoy shapes for identification, they carry the appropriate topmark where practicable, or lettered, the numbering or lettering follows the conventional direction of buoyage. Special marks, with can and conical shapes but painted yellow, may be used in conjunction with the standard lateral marks for special types of channel.

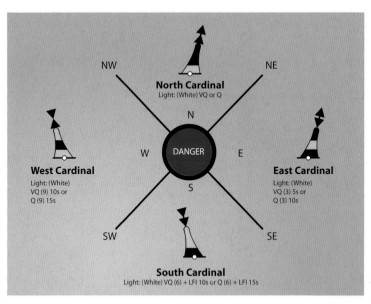

North Cardinal
Light: (White) VQ or Q

NW   NE

N

W   DANGER   E

S

West Cardinal
Light: (White)
VQ (9) 10s or
Q (9) 15s

East Cardinal
Light: (White)
VQ (3) 5s or
Q (3) 10s

SW   SE

South Cardinal
Light: (White) VQ (6) + LFl 10s or Q (6) + LFl 15s

Cardinal marks are used to tell you which side to leave dangers. For example, stay north of a North Cardinal mark to be safe.

The direction of buoyage

The direction of buoyage is shown by a large magenta arrow at various points on the chart.

This defines which side is port and starboard hand for the lateral markers when it is not obvious from the shape of the land.

The relationship between the chart and the way you interpret the buoys in the IALA-A and B regions is as shown opposite.

Direction of Buoyage

Buoyage

Depending where you are in the world the lateral markers, i.e. port and starboard hand markers, will be either the **IALA-A** or **IALA-B** system.

IALA-A is used by nations in Europe, Australia, New Zealand, parts of Africa and most of Asia other than the Philippines, Japan and Korea.

IALA-B is used by nations in North America, Central America and South America, the Philippines, Japan and Korea.

Buoyage in IALA-A regions

← Preferred Channels
← Secondary Channels

The Lateral Buoyage marking the channels is Red to Port, related to the Conventional Direction of Buoyage. Off the coast, the direction of buoyage in this area is from east to west; within the estuary, it is the direction taken by the mariner when approaching from seaward.

NOTE
The wreck is a New Danger, too recent to have been charted. See 1.17.

Racon D

(see Note)

N

REGION A
Examples of Buoyage

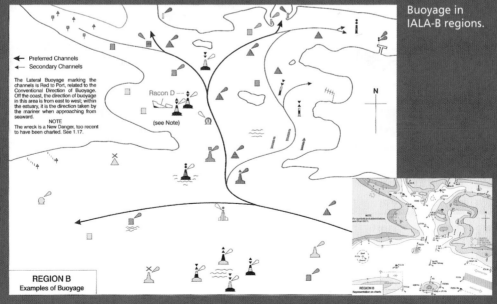

Buoyage in IALA-B regions.

← Preferred Channels
← Secondary Channels

The Lateral Buoyage marking the channels is Red to Port, related to the Conventional Direction of Buoyage. Off the coast, the direction of buoyage in this area is from east to west; within the estuary, it is the direction taken by the mariner when approaching from seaward.

NOTE
The wreck is a New Danger, too recent to have been charted. See 1.17.

Racon D

(see Note)

N

REGION B
Examples of Buoyage

Compass corrections

Magnetic compasses point to the magnetic north pole, but have some errors which have to be accounted for. These are magnetic **variation** (a global effect) and **deviation** (particular to each vessel).

Magnetic variation

Early mariners assumed that any compass pointed towards the North Pole and it was not until the early nineteenth century that navigators found that there are two north poles. The Magnetic North Pole is in Arctic Canada (82.7°N 114.4°W moving in a northwesterly direction in 2005). This angle between the True North and Magnetic North Poles has to be accounted for precisely. This correction angle is called Magnetic Variation.

There is similar variation between the South Magnetic Pole at approximately 64°S, 138°E, so if variation is west, then your compass needle points to the west of True North.

On Admiralty charts the size and change in time of the magnetic field is represented by a **compass rose**. The outer ring is aligned with True North and the inner ring with Magnetic North for the given year, in this case 2007. To calculate the variation for any given year, say 2009, you need to do the following:

12° 00'W 2007 (10'E) means that in 2007, the variation was exactly 12° W, decreasing by 10' annually, i.e. moving eastward by 10'E every year.

Variation in 2007 = 12° 00'W
Annual change   = 10'E
2 year's worth = 20'E
Variation in 2009 = 11° 40'W

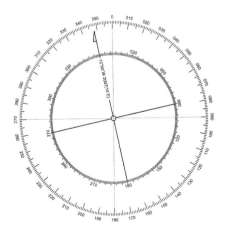

For yachting purposes, round this to the nearest degree.

Magnetic deviation

This is caused by ferrous items like the engine causing local distortions to the magnetic field near each compass. This effect changes with the vessel's heading too, since the relative positions of the metal object and the compass change within the magnetic field. It is good practice (and mandatory for commercially operated yachts) to have the compass checked and if necessary adjusted annually by a qualified compass adjuster. This is known as swinging the compass, and usually takes no more than a couple of hours.

The graph shows how deviation changes with the yacht's heading, and also how the deviation card, or compass card, is always a sinusoid. A good compass adjuster working with a good compass can get the deviation down to less than a couple of degrees.

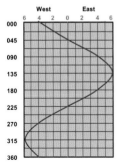

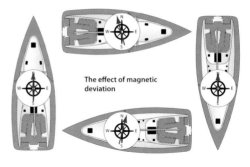

Ship's Head Compass (°C)	Deviation	Ship's Head Magnetic (°M)
000	4W	356
022.5	2W	020.5
045	0	045
067.5	2E	069.5
090	4E	094
112.5	5E	117.5
135	6E	141
157.5	5E	162.5
180	4E	184
202.5	2E	204.5
225	0	225
247.5	2W	245.5
270	4W	266
292.5	5W	287.5
315	6W	309
337.5	5W	332.5
360	4W	356

The effect of magnetic deviation

The degree of magnetic deviation is unique to each vessel and will vary according to its heading. Hence the need for a deviation card to correct the compass readings

Applying compass corrections

There are three type of compass heading:

Degrees True: with respect to **True North** – you put this on and measure it from the chart.

Degrees Magnetic: with respect to the Magnetic North Pole – if you had no ferrous objects on your vessel, this is what your compass would show due to the effect of **variation.**

Degrees Compass: this is what your compass actually reads due to variation and deviation. Here are two mnemonics:

TAWC: True Add West going towards Compass

CADET: Compass Add East going towards True

IMPORTANT – always note which type of degrees you are using, be it degT, degM or degC – this will save potentially dangerous misunderstandings.

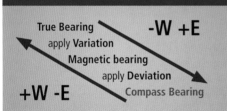

The **helmsman** always uses **degC**. It is the task of the **navigator to convert from degC and degT and visa-versa** though electronic chart plotters measure in either mode automatically

Who uses **degM**? Anyone taking bearings with a **hand-bearing compass**. Because these are not used in a fixed position on the yacht a deviation card cannot be drawn up, so take care to try and take bearings in a part of the yacht that is as ferrous-metal free as possible.

Compass heading example

It's important to have a system that you can depend on at 0230, when it's blowing a gale and you're feeling seasick. Let's say you want to steer 120°T, and it's 2009 and your deviation card is as shown above.

A chart plotter takes the headache out of these compass conversions, but as with any computer, garbage in translates to garbage out. It is important to know how to calculate true and magnetic bearings manually, so that electronic aberrations stand out like a sore thumb.

True →	Variation →	Magnetic →	Deviation →	Compass
120°T	12° W	132°M	6°E	126°C

You ask the helm to steer 126°C, and the reply comes back, 'Wind's shifted, I can only make 115°C'. You need to convert this to degT for the chart to see if this is safe and to plan around it. Use the same layout, just start from the other end – this ingrains the system.

True	← Variation	← Magnetic	← Deviation	← Compass
108° T	12° W	120° M	5° E	115° C

Assuming there is no leeway involved, this can now be plotted onto the chart and decisions made from there.

A little while later you decide to take a bearing on a lighthouse to check your progress, which is 050°M. This is done with the hand-bearing compass, and is therefore in degM. Treat this just as you did before:

True	← Variation	← Magnetic	← Deviation	← Compass
038° T	12° W	050° M		

And the true bearing of 038°T can now be plotted on the chart.

Checking your compass

It is easy to do an informal compass check by lining your yacht up with a known visible transit, such as a set of leading lights marking a harbour entrance. This is good to do on a regular basis, since it gives you confidence and acts as a check that no-one has done anything silly like leaving a toolbox in the cockpit locker next to the steering compass.

In this example, the bearing of the leading marks is 305°T, which is measured directly from

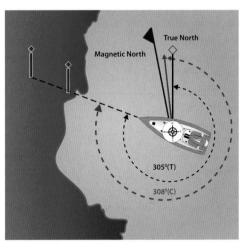

the chart. The compass heading is 308°C, which is read directly off the steering compass when the yacht is heading down the transit, and the variation is 12°W, calculated from the relevant compass rose on the chart. Following the previous example, all this is entered in the log.

True →	Variation →	Magnetic →	Deviation →	Compass
305°T	12° W	317° M	9° E	308° C

The deviation is the difference between degM and degC for that heading, in this case: 317°M – 308°C = 9°E of deviation.

Comparing this to the deviation card, it should be about 6°W for this heading.

Position fixing

To be a successful navigator, you have to be able to answer these two questions at all times: 'Where are we?' 'Where are we going?' and compare this to where you have been.

Fixes in general

A fix is a position on a chart 'fixed' by the intersection of two or more **position lines** which, as the name implies, means that you are somewhere on that line. The angle at which position lines intersect is called the **angle of cut**.

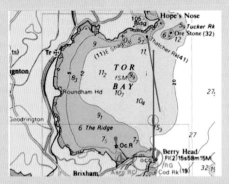

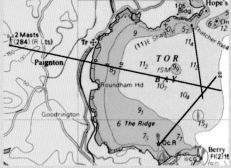

By taking bearings on *Thatcher Rock* and *Berry Head* the navigator has made a very poor fix, as the angle of cut is nearly 180° and so just a couple of degrees error (easy on a small moving yacht) gives a large uncertainty (shown by the hashed area).

This gives a much better angle of cut between the two position lines, and by adding the third position line, accuracy improves further.

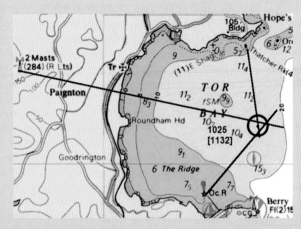

The **fix itself** is plotted as a circle with a point in the middle for the position, and every **fix** must have a **time** and a **log reading** next to it. The log reading is in brackets to differentiate between it and time – in this example the two could easily be confused. You should estimate the fix point closest to any dangers in your 'cocked hat' (the intersection of the various position lines). This plays it as safe as possible.

Satellite navigation system fixes

GPS satellite navigation systems are now an intergrated part of navigation. They must be looked at intelligently, since with all systems that depend on software algorithms they are only as good as the data put in. Here are a few things to watch for in your system set up:

Chart Datum: your GPS datum should be the same datum as that of the chart you are plotting the positions on.

Measurement units: check that your GPS is set to read out in nautical miles, knots and degrees true – these are all options.

Power supply: if hand-held, make sure you have enough batteries for the trip!

Aerial setup: make sure this is as per the manufacturer's recommendations and that the cable, if there is one, is secure. GPS signal problems often arise from a poorly fitted or deteriorating cable / aerial combination.

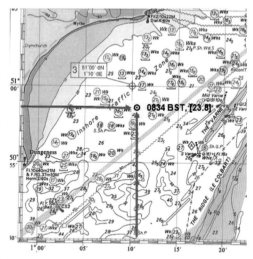

Once your plotter is set up correctly, you can take the latitude and longitude and plot these directly onto the chart. In this example the GPS position is 50°58.6'N, 001°10.7'E.

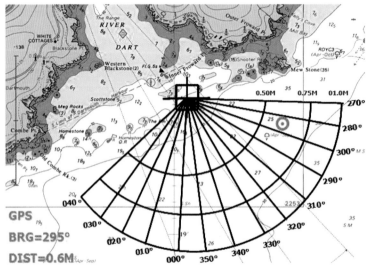

Waypoint web

This is a little time-consuming to draw up, but is excellent for high speed navigation.

By drawing the web relative to a waypoint that the GPS is programmed to, you have a very quick way of plotting your position.

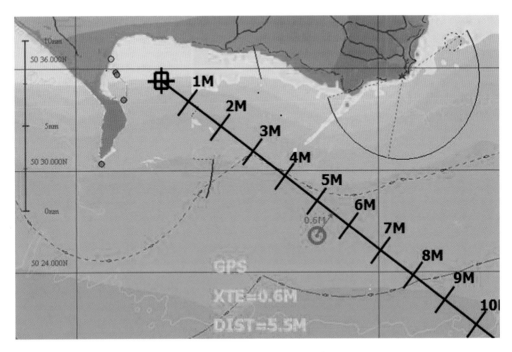

Cross track error ladder

Input two waypoints, and plot your position by distance to the destination waypoint, and XTE off the ideal track.

Electronic pilotage techniques

Clearing bearings

The clearing bearing of 255°T on the waypoint keeps you safe from the Mew Stone and other inshore rocks. Just so long as the Bearing To Waypoint is greater than 255°T, you are south of the line and therefore safe.

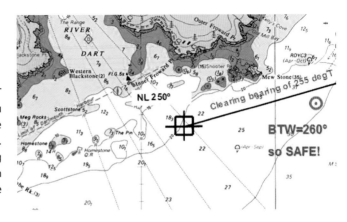

Distance off

By making a hazard into a waypoint and monitoring your distance to that waypoint, you can easily keep a safe distance off.

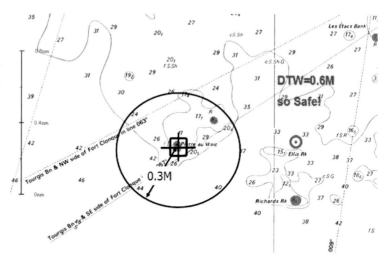

Cross track error

By setting 'no go' limits either side of the ideal track, you can use XTE to check you're not being swept to one side.

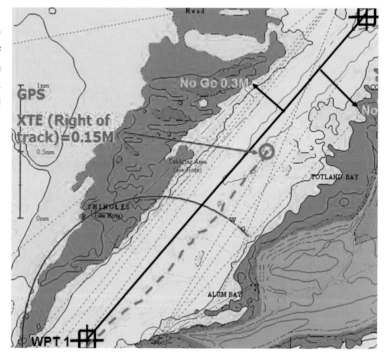

GPS for passage navigation

It is extremely important to make sure that all the waypoints are entered correctly, as a typo can have serious consequences. The major ones (50° S instead of 50° N) are fairly obvious, when you get a distance to waypoint of 12,000 nautical miles and you're only going on a weekend trip you'll notice it, but the relatively small errors that give you errors in heading of 15-20° are far more sneaky.

When planning a passage, the latitude and longitude for each waypoint has to be input with complete accuracy. The best way to check this is to compare the distance and bearings between waypoints, as calculated by the GPS, to those that you measured when you initially planned them on the chart. If all is well, they will correspond to a few tenths of a mile and a couple of degrees either way – if not, then check the waypoints on the GPS!

Visual fixes

These are taken using a combination of compass bearings, transits and depth soundings. Before going into detail, it is worth looking at what objects make good references or not.

Prominent fixed markers such as lighthouses, lit posts, church spires and headlands make excellent markers, as they do not move and are easily identifiable.

Major navigational buoys such as cardinal markers and lateral marks in busy commercial channels are also good, since they are unlikely to move. In areas of high tidal range be more careful, as their mooring chains allow significant sideways drift at low water.

Minor navigational markers such as yellow racing buoys and small lateral markers may be incorrect, their lights maybe not working, or they may just not be there at all.

> **Also, do ensure your charts are up to date!**

Three-point fixes

In the following example, you have taken a series of bearings with your hand-held, magnetic compass:

Radio Mast: 270°M; Water Tower 350°M; Church Spire 050°M

Variation is calculated as 3°W.

Convert these to degT to go on a chart. Remember the mnemonics, *TAWC* or *CADET* to decide whether to add or subtract variation.

True	← Variation	← Magnetic	← Deviation	← Compass
267° T	3° W	270° M	-	-
347°T	3° W	350° M	-	-
047°T	3°W	050°M	-	-

Unless conditions are perfect you will get a 'cocked hat' which effectively defines the potential error of the fix. It is prudent to put the fix closest to the nearest point of danger. Taking three bearings gives you much better control of visual inaccuracies.

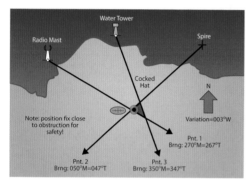

Transit fixes

These can be very useful. A transit is a line passing through two fixed objects, such as a set of leading lights, one set up behind another, as shown above by the markers leading into Nantucket. When these line up, and the **rear one** is **always highest,** you are on the transit, and this will be marked on the chart.

Equally useful are 'natural' transits, i.e. two specific charted objects coming in line so that you can draw the transit on the chart. These can be two headlands in line, or a church spire coming in line with a fixed post.

In the example, at 1542BST with a log reading of 45.8 miles, the lighthouse at *Le Stiff* lines up with the large beacon *Men Korn* to give a natural transit as a position line. There is no need to take bearings if you are sure of the identity of the two objects; all you need to

do is draw a line on the chart going through both of them. **At the same time** you take a bearing of 188°M on the large beacon *Les Trois Pierres.* Variation has previously been calculated as 7°W.

True	← Variation	← Magnetic	← Deviation	← Compass
181°T	7° W	188°M		

This can be plotted as shown and, as with every fix, the time and log reading is written on the chart.

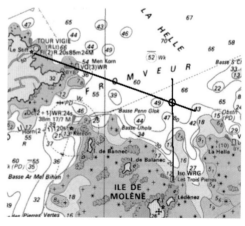

Using depth contours

Position lines don't have to be straight lines; they just have to be lines from which to check your position. Depth contours will often do for this. From a seamanship point of view, avoid using contours that pass near isolated rocks or are part of a steeply shoaling section, as this will give you very little margin for error. Looking at Tor Bay, the 10m contour in the southern and western parts of the bay is ideal, but along the north shore it gets very close to several rocks and an area of uncertain survey (dotted contour) so is unsuitable for safe navigation there.

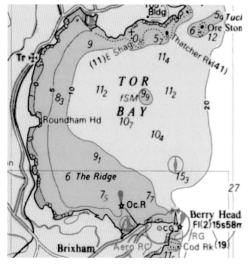

This technique does require you to know two things – the height of tide and the offset on your echo sounder. Many people like to set this so that the depth reads zero just as your keel touches bottom – this is entirely sensible, but does mean that you cannot read the water depth directly from the echo sounder.

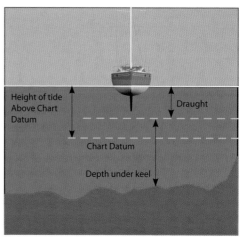

Assuming that the echo sounder is set to read zero at the bottom of the keel, then the calculation of the depth on a certain contour is as follows:

Work out the height of tide, and then:

Actual Water Depth for contour =
Contour Depth + Height of Tide
Echo sounder reading for contour =
Actual Water Depth – Draught

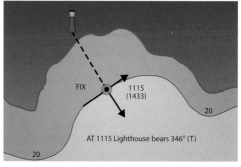

AT 1115 Lighthouse bears 346° (T)

This example shows how a contour can be combined with a bearing to give a reasonable fix.

Radar range fixes

If you have radar, this provides another way of position fixing that can be faster and more accurate than 3-point visual fixes. Small yacht radars are excellent for measuring range, but poor at measuring bearing. Also, radar ranges require identifiable features, so headlands with distinctive shapes and sheer cliffs are ideal – gradually sloping beaches are not, as they don't reflect the radar signal with any definition.

A simple method is to measure the range to a feature with radar, and then use your hand-bearing compass to take a bearing. Convert this to degrees True and you can plot this bearing, measure off the distance from the radar feature using a set of drawing compasses, and where they intersect is your fix.

The example here shows a **radar range** off the steep cliffs of Berry Head, and a **compass bearing** of the light at the end of the breakwater. This is another example of a position line not being a straight line.

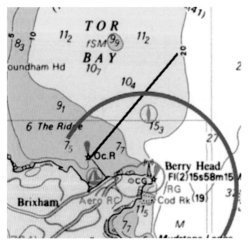

The wise navigator will use a range of navigations aids including a GPS plotter, depth sounder, compass as well as radar to plot a fix and track their course. A sister companion, *Essential Boat Radar* by Bill Johnson provides a comprehensive overview.

Tidal flow calculation

Tidal stream atlases

These are the most visually obvious sources of tidal flow data, and are good sources for most situations, showing eddies and counter currents well. Each tidal stream atlas covers a specific area, for example Admiralty Publication NP264, The Channel Islands and Adjacent Coasts of France. This has a separate page for each hour of tide, going from 6 hours before High Water to 6 hours after High Water. The High Water reference is that of Dover. It is important to **carefully check which port is the reference port,** as it differs for each atlas and may not even be on the area covered by the atlas, as in this case.

If we wanted to see what the tide was doing in the Little Russel between Guernsey and Herm after 0900 UT on Saturday, 7 February 2009, for example, we first need to see where we are in relation to HW Dover. The tidal data for Dover on this day is

Dover Sat 7 Feb 2009	LW	0342 UT	1.69m
	HW	0855 UT	5.91m
	LW	1624 UT	1.51m

Starting at the HW page, write (in pencil!) the time of HW Dover at the top, as shown.

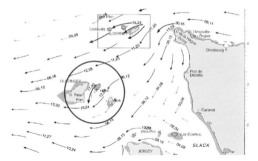 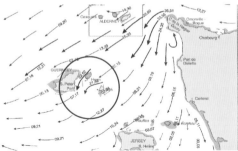

This page is valid from half an hour before HW Dover to half an hour after, i.e. 0825 to 0925UT. Alongside, the 1 hour AFTER HW Dover page, write HW Dover + 1, and carry on with this until the overall time for the planned journey is done.

This page is now valid from 0925 until 1025, when the 2 hours AFTER HW Dover page starts. In the Little Russel at 0900, therefore, the tide is represented by an arrow. The numbers represent the rates in tenths of a knot at Mean Neap and Mean Spring tides respectively, i.e. 1.7 knots at neaps, 4.0 knots at springs.

At the front of each tidal stream atlas and in each local almanac is a Computation of Rates table, which allows you to work out tidal flow rates when you're not exactly at springs or neaps. The basic principle behind this is that the greater the RANGE of tide that day (up the vertical axis), the greater the RATE will be (along the horizontal axis), as there is more water to flow in and out in the same time between high and low water. At Dover in the morning of Saturday, February 7, 2009 the range of tide is **Range = HW – LW = 5.91m – 1.51m = 4.4m**

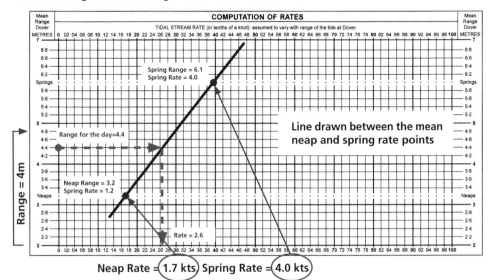

Do extend the line past the neap and spring lines – these are MEAN values, and if you have a high spring or a low neap you will need to go above or below the lines.

The interpolated **rate** is therefore 2.6 knots, and the **direction** is taken directly from the arrow. Remember – this is **only valid for the hour covered by each page,** and you need to be on the right page for the right time.

These are another representation of tidal data, designated on the charts as magenta diamonds, to provide the tidal stream data at a particular point.

Tidal diamonds

This example is from Admiralty Chart Number 5606.1, Southern North Sea and Dover Strait. The reference port is DOVER. Each column is a particular diamond, and gives its latitude and longitude – for example 50° 56.2'N, 1° 16.7' for diamond A.

TIDAL INFORMATION

5606·1 Tidal Streams referred to HW at DOVER

Hours	Geographical Position	Directions of streams (degrees)	Rates at spring tides (knots)	Rates at neap tides (knots)	Ⓐ 50°56·2N 1 16·7E		Ⓑ 50°59·9N 1 34·0E		Ⓒ 51°26·0N 1 38·9E		Ⓓ 51 1	
Before High Water 6					233	2·2 1·2	260	1·8 1·2	137	0·5 0·3	231	1·
5					232	2·5 1·4	260	2·6 1·8	164	1·1 0·6	218	2
4					233	2·1 1·2	260	2·9 2·0	173	1·6 0·9	213	2
3					232	0·9 0·5	260	2·7 1·9	189	1·9 1·1	206	2·
2					050	0·4 0·2	270	1·2 0·8	201	1·5 0·8	207	1·
1					052	1·2 0·7	035	0·8 0·5	240	0·7 0·4	053	0
High Water					058	2·6 1·5	060	1·7 1·1	328	1·0 0·5	040	1·
After High Water 1					052	2·3 1·3	060	2·5 1·7	353	1·5 0·8	035	2·
2					052	1·8 1·0	060	2·6 1·8	004	1·6 0·9	040	2·
3					055	1·0 0·6	060	1·9 1·3	016	1·3 0·7	030	1·
4						0·0 0·0	053	0·8 0·5	026	1·0 0·5	023	1·
5					232	0·8 0·4	277	0·5 0·6	044	0·6 0·3	345	0·
6					232	1·8 1·0	260	1·9 1·3	107	0·3 0·2	246	0·

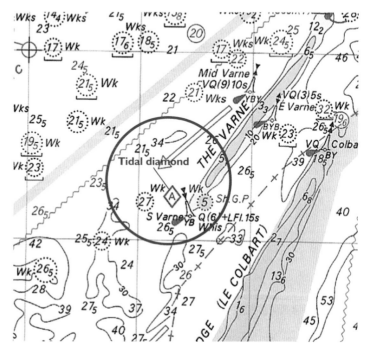

When we want to know what the tide was doing at diamond A at 0930UT on Wednesday, 11 February 2009, we need to reference this to the tide at Dover, obtained from the Almanac.

Dover Wed, 11 Feb 2009	LW 0733UT	0.46m
	HW 1218UT	6.74m
	LW 1959T	0.65m

Organisation is key, since being an hour out can completely change things. Start by seeing whether you are before or after HW. In this case, it is before.

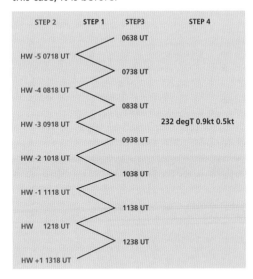

STEP 1: Make a zigzag ladder up the page, giving yourself two lines per complete zigzag.
STEP 2: Start with the HW time down towards the bottom, and write down the times of HW-1,-2,-3, etc. up the page until you are definitely past the times required.

STEP 3: On the other side of the zigzag, put the times of the start and finish of each of the tidal hours, i.e. 30 minutes before and after the hour time.
STEP 4: Look at the tidal hour start and finish times, and decide in which hour your time fits – in this case 0930UT is in the HW-3 hour, from 0838UT to 0938. The tidal diamond table shows that for diamond A at HW-3 the tide is setting at 232°T, with 0.9kts at mean springs, and 0.5kts at mean neaps.

Now all you need to do is go back to the Computation of Rates table as before (page 155) to interpolate between springs and neaps.

Logbooks, dead reckoning and estimated position – keeping track of progress

To keep a good handle on where you are, it is vital to record all the information in order to be able to reconstruct your track on the chart from your last known point, your last fix.

The logbook

The ship's log is an important legal document. Apart from navigational information, it is the place to record who you have on board and in what capacity, any standing orders, weather forecasts received, and details of any incidents; indeed anything to do with the daily running of your yacht.

Navigationally, it is your primary data repository for where you've taken your yacht and what the conditions were like. Log entries should be made:

• On the hour;
• When the course changes on passage;

- When an evolution occurs on deck;
- Record radio traffic involving your yacht;
- When any incident or accident occurs;
- Weather reports hourly
- Position reports half-hourly

If you are short tacking up a river, for example, it is not possible to record every course change, so there is an element of practicality involved. A recommendation would be to record the start and finish of it. For example:

1500: Started MOB drills with new crew in open water 1 mile west of harbour entrance; 1545: Finished drills. On passage now.

There are many good logbooks available. Make sure the data columns cover everything you want. The important ones are:

Navigational data:

Time: Usually local time is most convenient. If you're on an ocean passage you may find it convenient to keep time in UT – this is an entirely personal choice. The important thing is to record what time you are using.

Time	Course steered (°C)	Deviation	Variation	True Course (°T)	Log Reading	Position (GPS)
1100 BST	260° C	3° W	3° W	254°T	1106.8	Lat/long
1200 BST	280° C	6° W	3° W	271°T	1114.9	Lat/long

Course steered: This is what the helm has been steering **since the last log entry** – it may well be different to what the helm was asked to steer! It is important to know what has actually happened. In this case the course steered was 260°C until 1100BST when it was changed to 280°C.

Deviation & variation: Obtained from the yacht's deviation card and the chart respectively.

True course: This can be used on the chart.

Log reading: Taken directly from the yacht's instruments, ideally to the nearest cable (tenth of a nautical mile).

Position: Taken from your hourly fix, usually a GPS reading.

Weather and conditions:

True wind direction: If your instruments are calibrated correctly you will be able to obtain this there, otherwise it's a case of visual observation. The example above shows why the course has changed – the wind veered 20°, and so the helm had to follow it.

True wind speed: Ideally from properly calibrated instruments, otherwise observation and experience.

Leeway: The amount your yacht is pushed sideways by the wind.

Barometer: A very important weather forecasting tool. In this case it is dropping steadily. Don't tap barometers – that just puts in an incorrect offset.

Sea state: From observation.

Cloud cover: Given in oktas – coverage of the sky from one eighth to eight eighths.

True Wind Direction	True Wind Speed	Leeway	Barometer	Sea State	Cloud Cover	Weather/ Visibility
200°T	20 kts	7°	1003	Moderate	6/8	Showers/moderate
220°T	22 kts	7°	1002	Moderate	8/8	Squalls/mod or poor in squalls

Weather/visibility: By observation – are you getting wet, and if so how much? Include temperature.

These observations give an overall picture of the weather. In this case it is deteriorating, but not rapidly. By comparing it with a previous forecast and ideally a synoptic chart, you can make an informed opinion about the weather systems, and whether it is safe to continue or not.

Vessel & voyage information:

Power	Sail plan	Notes
No	2 reefs, ½ head	Bouncy. Jim recovered from seasickness. Eddystone Lighthouse sighted off starboard beam, bears 355°M.
No	3 reefs ⅓ head	Shortened sail for squalls. Still bouncy. Jim on helm with big grin.

Power: Is the engine on? If so what for, and at what revs? It could be on to charge batteries, for example.

Sail plan: Taken in conjunction with the overall weather, this gives an idea of the yacht's motion.

Notes: Whatever is relevant – dolphins sighted, for example.

Leeway

Leeway is the amount that a yacht is pushed off its heading by the wind and the sideways force generated by the sails. The factors to take into consideration include the strength of the wind, its direction relative to the yacht's heading and the design characteristics of the yacht. Deep-draught, long keeled-yachts do not get pushed sideways anywhere near as much as flat-bottomed, shallow draught-vessels.

The relative direction of the wind is very important. When sailing close-hauled, a significant portion of the drive of the sails is sideways and can push the yacht off its compass course by up to 15-20°. When assessing leeway, use the heel angle of your yacht as a guide – the more the heel, the more the sideways force on the yacht and the more leeway you have. Obviously, this is not a good indicator for catamarans. Instead look back at your wake. The difference in direction between the line of the wake and the centreline of the yacht is the amount of leeway you have. From a performance point of view, this is another reason not to sail over-canvassed when close-hauled – it may be really exciting and feel very fast to have the toe rail buried under the waves, but in reality you are making far more leeway than you would if you took a reef in.

Leeway is always put onto the TRUE heading of the yacht, and not the course heading through the water. Whether you add it on or take it off depends on the relative direction of the wind. It is good to make a drawing of the situation.

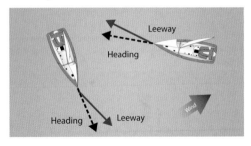

In the case of the yacht (right) the heading is 280°T, close-hauled on port tack. The yacht will be pushed away from the wind, so leeway (in this case say 8°) needs to be ADDED to the heading to give the true course of 288°T, which can now be plotted on the chart.

In the second example (left), the yacht is now on starboard tack in the same SW wind, with a heading of 170°T. The yacht is being pushed away from the wind, so the 8° of leeway needs to be SUBTRACTED, giving a true course of 162°T which can be plotted on the chart.

A general rule:

STARBOARD SUBTRACT, PORT ADD.

Dead Reckoning (DR) - The most basic guess

This allows you to plot the yacht's position taking account of its relative movement through the water. In the example below, only the log book columns essential to this are shown.

5° leeway on STARBOARD tack SUBTRACT **075°T on chart**

Time	Course° C)	Log	Wind	Leeway	Position	Comment
1230UT	Pilotage	102.3	SE f5	5°	0.5 M N of breakwater	Out of harbour, onto course of 080° C
1300 UT	080° C	105.5	SE f5	5°	DR	Still close hauled on starboard tack

True	← Variation	← Magnetic	← Deviation	← Compass	True →	Variation →	Magnetic →	Deviation →	Compass
080°T	3°W	083°M	3°E	080°C	305°T	12°W	317°M	9°E	308°C

Track length = Log at 1300 – log at 1230 = 3.2 nautical miles
The fix is plotted, and then the track, including leeway plotted from that initial fix. The DR is denoted by a dash across the track at the relevant point, and has the time and log reading next to it. Since this is the **water track**, it is denoted by 1 arrowhead, as shown below.

Time	Course° C)	Log	Wind	Leeway	Position	Comment
1230UT	Pilotage	102.3	SE f5	5°	0.5 M N of breakwater	Out of harbour, onto course of 080°C
1300 UT	080° C	105.5	SE f5	5°	DR	Still close-hauled on starboard tack

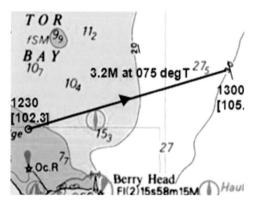

Estimated Positions (EP's)

This is the most educated estimate of the yacht's position in the water.

Effectively, an EP is a DR with tidal set and drift added on. Using the previous example of a DR:

5° leeway on STARBOARD tack SUBTRACT **075°T on chart**

True	← Variation	← Magnetic	← Deviation	← Compass
080°T	3°W	083°M	3°E	080°C

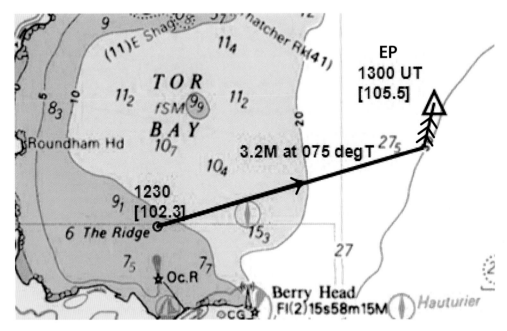

Track length = Log at 1300 – Log at 1230 = 3.2 nautical miles

Looking at the chart shows that tidal diamond B is close by. Using this as shown on page 156 you calculate that the tidal flow for this period of time, 1230UT to 1300UT is 0.5 knots towards 010°T. So to complete the EP, plot the DR as before and then add the tidal vector to it. The tidal vector is denoted by three arrow heads, and the EP is shown as a triangle.

Plotting a course to steer

So far, we have discussed where we are and where we have been. Of equal importance is where we are going, and how to allow for tide and leeway to calculate the shortest course between two places.

You are at the position marked on the chart below, and want to navigate to a position half a mile due south of Thatcher Rock to give you a safe approach into the delights of Torquay. With the current conditions (fine reach on starboard tack) the estimated boat speed will be 5.5 knots, with 6° of leeway, and variation is 3° W. The procedure is as follows:

1. Draw the **projected ground track** to the destination and beyond, and measure the distance to travel – in this case 6.0 nautical miles.

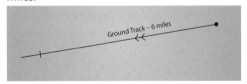

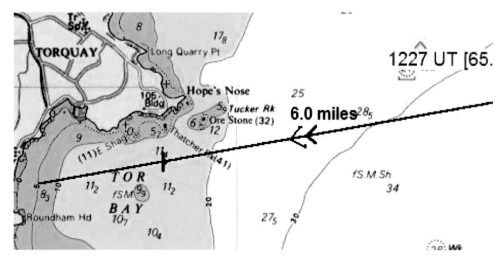

2. Calculate the approximate time for the journey – it's 6 miles long and our boat speed is 5.5 knots, so it will take just over an hour or so. This is an estimate only, and allows us to work out the period of time over which to calculate the tide.

Dover Sat 7 Feb 2009	LW	0342UT	1.69m
	HW	0855UT	5.91m
	LW	1624UT	1.51m

By using the method on page 170 it gives you 4 hours after HW Dover as the main part of the journey.

Now plot the tidal vector for the time period of your journey. Make it easy by using full distances. The triangle on the chart finishes

before the destination. This means that it will take slightly more than an hour to get to Torquay.

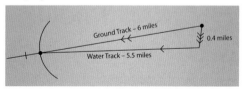

Journey times and estimated times of arrival

To estimate times, you must work with the ground track. Charts are compiled with respect to land, and your arrival and destination points are plotted likewise. So, too, must be your speed, distance and time calculations. There is one basic equation:

$$\text{Speed} = \frac{\text{Distance}}{\text{Time}}$$

This makes sense when you think about knots – nautical miles per hour, or distance over time.

To juggle these three quantities around, remember the DST triangle: Cover up the one you want, and the other two are given.

Cover up	Speed =	$\dfrac{\text{Distance}}{\text{Time}}$
Cover up	Time =	$\dfrac{\text{Distance}}{\text{Speed}}$
Cover up	Distance =	Speed x Time

Remember – everything here is with respect to the ground, so you need to use SOG – speed over ground – in all the calculations.

Referring to the previous example, the length of the ground track from the start point to the interception of the water track (the interception is shown in red) is 5.7 miles.

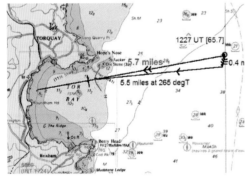

This means that the ground track is 5.7 nautical miles long over a period of one hour.

Speed Over Ground

SOG = Distance / time

= 5.7 miles/ 1 hour

SOG = 5.7 knots

The distance of the journey is 6.0 nautical miles, measured in Step 1 of Course to Steer.

Time = Distance/Speed

Time = $\dfrac{\text{Distance to destination}}{\text{Speed Over Ground}}$

= $\dfrac{6.0 \text{ miles}}{5.7 \text{ knots}}$

= 1.05 hours

Time = 1 hour 3 minutes

The time of the fix was 1227UT, so

Estimated Time of Arrival (ETA)

= Start time + journey time

ETA = 1227UT + 1 hour 3 minutes

ETA = 1330UT

Relationship between water track and ground track

This somewhat daunting phrase sums up the relationship between the yacht's motion through the water **(water track)**, the water's motion over the ground **(tidal set, or direction – and drift, or rate)** and the yacht's motion over the ground **(ground track)**.

Each of these tracks is defined by a speed and a direction. These are all expressed in **knots and degrees True.**

Water track: Defined by **heading (including leeway)** and **log speed**

Tide track: Defined by **set** and **drift**

Ground track: Defined by **course over ground (COG) and speed over ground (SOG)**

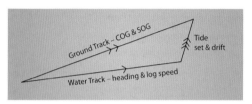

The ground track is the result of drawing the water track and adding the tide track to the end of it, just like doing an EP. It is essential that **all three tracks have the same time period.**

Water track: One arrow (1 bow wave per hull)

Ground track: Two arrows (2 footprints on the ground)

Tide track: Three arrows,

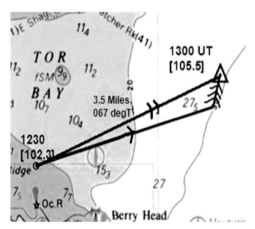

Looking at the EP worked through in the previous section, the triangle can be completed as shown.

Each side of this triangle is over half an hour of time. The ground track is 3.5 miles long, with a bearing of 067°T. **This is the track along which the yacht has moved,** even though its course through the water was 075°T. Hence:

Course Over Ground (COG) = 067°T

As it has travelled 3.5 miles in 30 minutes, over 60 minutes it would travel 2 x 3.5 = 7 miles.

7 miles in 1 hour give a **Speed Over Ground (SOG) of 7 knots.**

The running fix

This is a useful technique for taking a visual fix while running down the coast and only one identifiable object can be seen at a time – when the weather is hazy and you only have two to three miles visibility.

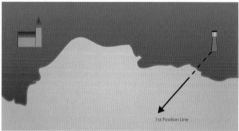

The diagram shows a visible lighthouse, with the church not yet in sight. Take a bearing of the lighthouse. After converting it to degrees True, plot that on the chart. All you know for sure is that you are somewhere on this line; you can use other data to give a better idea (for example depth), but this is the only decent bit of data you have at the time.

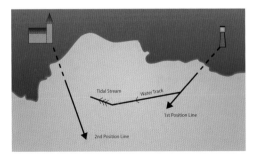

Guesstimating your position on the first position line, you continue down the coast until you can take a bearing on the church. Convert it to degrees True and plot it on the chart, as well as an EP from your guesstimated position on the first position line.

You know three things: you **were** on the first position line, you **are** on the second, and you **have moved** as defined by your EP between the two.

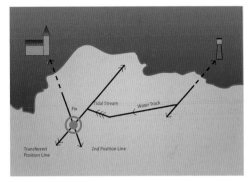

By transferring your first position line, which means taking the bearing of the first object, the lighthouse, and drawing that across the end of your EP, you will find that crosses the second position line – this is your fix!

'Where am I?' and 'Where am I going?' – The 6 minute rule

Picture the scene – it's 0245 Summer Time. You are beating up the eastern Solent, into a rather pleasant 10 knot westerly breeze with an ebb tide beneath you, heading for a marina in Cowes. A few miles out, you decide to do the rest of it under engine to give you time to tidy up, and go for the starter button. Nothing happens.

Not a problem, you can continue sailing, and there are lots of mooring buoys to sail onto in order to sort the engine out, so you carry on tacking upwind. The Solent is well lit, you know that just so long as you avoid rough water and keep a good eye out for the lights marking the Brambles Bank you won't run aground anywhere. So, apart from popping up every few minutes to check where you are, and keeping a good lookout (including a glance under the headsail), you don't worry too much about the navigation. So far so good. But then, suddenly an unlit yellow racing marker whizzes by frighteningly close to the leeward side.

The big problem is that while you've been doing all sorts of useful things, you have only ever answered the question 'Where WAS I?', instead of the really important questions, 'Where AM I?' and 'Where am I GOING?'. The 6 minute rule is an easy, quick and accurate way of doing that, and after very little practice it takes seconds to use.

Why 6 minutes? It's one tenth of an hour, which makes the sums easy, especially at 0245 whilst heeling over. A bit of preparation is needed for this, so let's go through it all from the start, taking the above example.
Portsmouth:

0159UTC 0259BST	4.5m	
0721UTC 0821BST	1.1m	
Range	**3.4m so 75% Springs.**	

The edge of your plotter is a good tool for working this one out. In your navigation notebook, draw a line and mark out the spring and neap ranges on it (from the Portsmouth tidal curve, in this case). The actual range is three quarters of the way from the neap range to the spring range, and an eyeball estimation will give you reasonable accuracy.

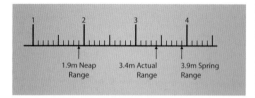

1.9m Neap   3.4m Actual   3.9m Spring
Range   Range   Range

The next step is to have the tidal stream atlas (or diamonds) labelled up with the correct times. This should be done anyway prior to arriving in the area covered by the atlas. This allows you to see at a glance what the tide is doing. In this example, we see:

So, we can interpolate 75% of springs to be about 1.6kts, or, by using the plotter method, also about 1.6 kts.

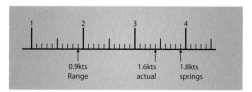

0.9kts   1.6kts   1.8kts
Range   actual   springs

In practice an eyeball interpolation will get you to within 0.2 kts of the theoretically correct figure. This is all the preparation work you need – so far a couple of minutes at most.

You now have a line on the chart which tells you where you ARE and where you're GOING at any given time, as opposed to just a fix, which only tells you where you WERE. The beauty is that the only maths you've needed is to divide a number by 10 – with no awkward speed/time/distance calculations to be done.

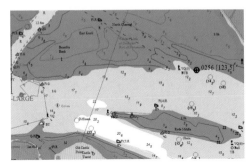

This is your starting point – a fix at 0256 BST.

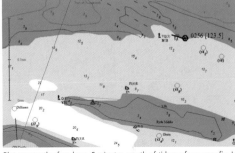

Plot one tenth of an hour, 6 minutes, worth of tide on from your fix. In this case that's 0.16 miles.

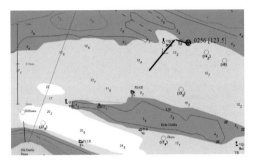

Since you are sailing to windward you don't have the luxury of choosing your course, so you ask the helm what he is steering – '235 on the compass at about 5 knots' comes the reply. After taking into account variation, deviation and leeway, this is plotted, again using one tenth of an hour's worth of water track, i.e. 0.5 of a mile.

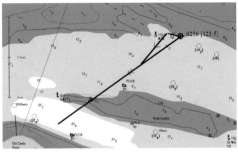

Measure the length of the ground track between your fix and the end of the water track, and walk the dividers along the ground track, marking off the notches. Each one represents 6 minutes worth of your boat's track over the ground. However, you are doing just over 6 knots of ground speed.

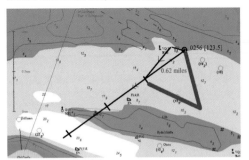

Now you can work out your ground track, by extrapolating from your fix through the end of the water track and as far out as is necessary, as shown below. This shows that you're heading for the unlit yellow racing buoy 'SL', now you need to know how much time you've got.

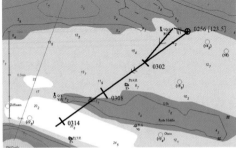

So, the last bit of chart work is to label each notch. From this, you can see, by eyeballing the ground track, that you will be abeam the Fl(4)R port-hand marker at about 0305, and getting perilously close to the unlit yellow at about 0309.

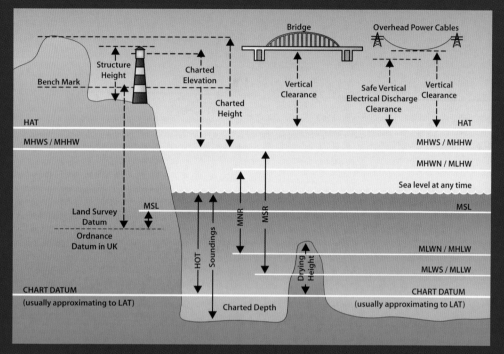

Tidal heights

In many parts of the world these are very significant, with tidal ranges (the difference between high and low water) being in the order of 15m. There are a few definitions, best illustrated by a diagram.

Chart Datum: the **vertical** datum. All drying heights and depths are referenced to this, and this is the point of zero tidal height.

LAT: Lowest Astronomical Tide. This is close to, but not necessarily equal to Chart Datum. For example, London Bridge at very low spring tides occasionally has -0.1m of tide.

MLWS: Mean Low Water Springs, sometimes found as Mean Low Low Water (MLLW). Spring lows can be lower than this; it is a mean, or average, figure.

MLWN: Mean Low Water Neaps, sometimes found as Mean High Low Water (MHLW). This is an average; very 'neapy' neaps can have higher low waters.

Sea Level: This is Chart Datum plus the Height of tide. This is the actual water depth at any given time.

MHWN: Mean High Water Neaps, sometimes found as Mean Low High Water (MLHW).

MHWS: Mean High Water Springs, sometimes found as Mean High High Water (MHHW).

HAT: Highest Astronomical Tide.

Tide tables

Almanacs and local pilot guides give tide tables for any standard port at any day of the year. These tables give the times and heights of the low and high waters each day. As well as providing HW and LW times and heights, the tables also give information about the Moon, and whether you are at springs, neaps, or, as is more likely, somewhere in between. The 9 of February has a white circle next to it, signifying a full moon, and the 25th a black circle, signifying a new moon. About a day or so after these, the HW and LW marks are at their most extreme, in other words at springs. On the 2nd and 16th of February there is a half moon, and a day or so after, the HW and LW marks are closest together, indicating neap tides.

You will invariably need to calculate tidal heights in between HW and LW, and for that you need the tidal curve, shown below for Portsmouth. The curve shows the tide rising up from LW to a peak at HW, then falling off towards the next LW. Each tidal curve is different, and depends on the local geography and topography of the sea bed. Portsmouth is in the semi-enclosed waters of the Solent, and has quite different flow

High & low water at Falmouth FEBRUARY 2009
See inside front cover for time factors for other ports

Time	m	Time	m	Time	m	Time
1 0242 0836 SU 1505 2056	1.3 4.9 1.3 4.7	**9** 0448 1137 M 1721 O 2357	5.4 0.6 5.2 0.6	**17** 0410 0948 TU 1632 2213	1.8 4.4 2.0 4.3	**25** 0526 1210 W 1750 ●
2 0318 0915 M 1544 ☽ 2140	1.5 4.8 1.5 4.6	**10** 0536 1225 TU 1809	5.6 0.3 5.4	**18** 0501 1041 W 1732 2323	2.2 4.0 2.3 4.1	**26** 0022 0604 TH 1243 1826
3 0403 1008 TU 1636 2242	1.6 4.6 1.8 4.4	**11** 0042 0624 W 1308 1853	0.4 5.7 0.2 5.4	**19** 0617 1218 TH 1854	2.4 3.9 2.5	**27** 0054 0640 F 1313 1859
4 0507 1121 W 1752	1.9 4.3 2.0	**12** 0123 0707 TH 1347 1932	0.3 5.7 0.3 5.3	**20** 0120 0751 F 1407 2035	4.1 2.4 4.0 2.3	**28** 0123 0713 SA 1343 1929
5 0004 0645 TH 1250 1936	4.3 2.1 4.3 2.0	**13** 0200 0745 F 1423 2005	0.5 5.5 0.5 5.2	**21** 0234 0927 SA 1506 2148	4.3 2.0 4.3 1.9	
6 0135 0828 F 1420 2104	4.4 1.9 4.4 1.7	**14** 0233 0818 SA 1454 2033	0.7 5.3 0.9 5.0	**22** 0325 1018 SU 1553 2234	4.6 1.6 4.6 1.5	
7 0253 0945 SA 1533 2212	4.7 1.5 4.7 1.4	**15** 0304 0844 SU 1524 2058	1.1 5.0 1.3 4.8	**23** 0409 1058 M 1634 2313	4.9 1.3 4.8 1.3	
8 0356 1046 SU 1631 2308	5.1 1.0 5.0 0.9	**16** 0335 0912 M 1554 ☾ 2129	1.5 4.7 1.6 4.5	**24** 0448 1135 TU 1711 2349	5.1 1.1 4.9 1.1	

All times are U.T.

regimes for flooding and ebbing tides. Also given in the title box are the mean Spring and Neap ranges – allowing you to decide which of the curves to use, or how far in between them to interpolate.

If the range is 3.9m, then use the Springs curve for Portsmouth; if 1.9m the Neaps, and if 2.9m, draw a curve half way between.

Some ports have Low Water curves. This happens when the HW is not well defined, usually in semi-enclosed waters. Southampton is one example.

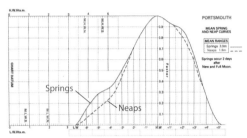

Interpolate for tides between neaps and springs.

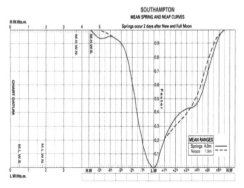

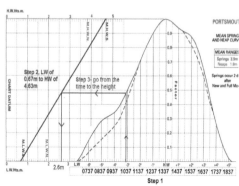

Working out the height of tide for a given time

Using Friday, 13 February 2009 as an example, the tidal data for Portsmouth is:

Portsmouth, 13 Feb 2009		
HW	0129UT	4.75m
LW	0649UT	0.67m
HW	1337UT	4.63m
LW	1907UT	0.59m

To calculate the height of tide at 1030UT:

Step 1: Fill out the time boxes, with the relevant HW as a reference. Each time written is the middle of the hour for that box, and each small subdivision is 10 minutes.

Step 2: Draw the height line from the LW value to the HW value, and note the range (in this case Range = 4.63m – 0.67m = 3.96m).

Step 3: Enter the time axis at the desired time, go up to the relevant curve, which in this case, is the Springs one since the range for the day is very close to the mean Springs range. Go across to the height line, and read off the height of tide – 2.6m

The procedure is the same when using a Low Water curve, except that you use a LW time in the centre of the time boxes. You do this when planning the time to leave a marina with a tidal sill, or if you have beached your catamaran overnight and need to work out what time she will afloat in the morning.

Take the situation where you need to dry out your yacht to paint her bottom in Southampton. You are able to start work once the height of tide gets below 2.5m. You need to calculate the available window.

The tide tables for Southampton give you:

13 Feb 2009			
	LW	0655UT	0.4m
	HW	1310UT	4.7m
	LW	1913UT	0.4m
14 Feb 2009			
	HW	0134UT	4.4m

For an online worldwide tide calculator visit:
http://easytide.ukho.gov.uk

Using the method opposite and entering the desired 2.5m height of tide, go to the rising height curve, which is a Spring curve due to the range. The time can be read off as 2343UT - time to put down the brushes!

Secondary ports

If every single port had its own tide tables and curve then it would mean that you'd have to buy massive tomes of nautical almanacs to have all that data. A way of getting round this is to designate the main ports as **standard ports**, and have all the minor ones in the area refer to their particular standard port with some corrections. These are **secondary ports.**

Secondary ports use the **same tidal curve as their standard port**, and need adjusted times and heights to make them work.

Plymouth, 13 Feb 2009:		
LW	0212UT	0.5 m
HW	0812UT	5.7 m
LW	1433UT	0.6 m
HW	2032UT	5.4 m

To make the tidal curve work we need a HW time for the middle of the time axis, and a LW and HW height. It is a good idea to make a table up to remind yourself of this, as it will prevent you from converting numbers that you don't need.

	HW time	HW height	LW height (1)	LW height (2)
Standard Port	0812UT	5.7m	0.5m	0.6m
Difference				
Secondary Port				
Summer time?				

TORQUAY Standard Port PLYMOUTH							
Times				Heights in Metres			
High Water		Low Water		MHWS	MHWN	MLWN	MLWS
0100	0600	0100	0600	5.5	4.4	2.2	0.8
1300	1800	1300	1800				
+0025	+0045	+0010	0000	-0.4	-0.9	-0.4	-0.1

Each secondary port has a table in the almanac giving the required information, as shown for Torquay below. This converts the Plymouth heights and times into Torquay heights and times. Say you want to use the tidal curve for Torquay for the morning of Friday, 13 February 2009.

As the standard port is Plymouth, write down the Plymouth tidal information.

To convert the times, look at the conversion table for high water times.

Times
High Water
0100   0600
1300   1800
———————————
+0025   +0045

This means that if HW Plymouth was either 0100 or 1300, if you add 25 minutes, you get HW Torquay. Similarly, if HW Plymouth was either 0600 or 1800, you add 45 minutes to get HW Torquay.

If the HW height was exactly 5.5m, i.e MHWS, then the correction would be -0.4 and HW Torquay at MHWS would be 5.1m. Usually interpolation is required.

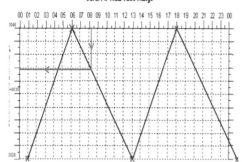

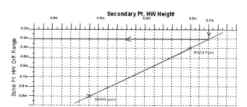

In this example, the standard port HW height is above the MHWS mark, so the line between the MHWS and MHWN points must be extended. This gives a correction of -0.3m.

In this case, we need only to convert one time, 0812UT. That is shown in the diagram above, and gives a correction of +0039 minutes, and a HW Torquay of 0851UT.

	HW time	HW height	LW height (1)	LW height (2)
Standard Port	0812UT	5.7m	0.5m	0.6m
Difference	+0039			
Secondary Port	0851UT			
Summer time?	No			

The HW height is converted using a similar process.

	HW time	HW height	LW height (1)	LW height (2)
Standard Port	0812UT	5.7m	0.5m	0.6m
Difference	+0039	-0.3m		
Secondary Port	0851UT	5.4m		
Summer time?	No			

It doesn't matter which way round the axes on the graph go, or where each axis starts.

The LW heights are done in the same way. The reason that we are doing two LW heights is that the tide comes up from the previous LW to the central HW and down to the following LW, and we want to look at the tide for the entire morning. Depending on what tidal data you want, you may only have to do one HW and one LW.

Heights in Metres

MHWS	MHWN
5.5	4.4
-0.4	-0.9

Heights in Metres

MLWN	MLWS
2.2	0.8
-0.4	-0.1

Looking at the LW column, when the standard port LW is 2.2m, i.e MLWN, the correction is -0.4m. When it is at 0.8m, i.e MLWS, the correction is -0.1m.

As the Standard Port LW is below MLWS, the line is extended as before. This gives the final two corrections. It doesn't matter which way round the axes on the graph go, or where each axis starts.

	HW time	HW height	LW height (1)	LW height (2)
Standard Port	0812UT	5.7m	0.5m	0.6m
Difference	+0039	-0.3m	+0.1m	+0.1m
Secondary Port	0851UT	5.4m	0.6m	0.7m
Summer time?	No			

(For standard port curve see page 170)

This can now be used just as any other tidal curve. It is no longer a Plymouth curve, and therefore the Plymouth mean spring and neap ranges no longer apply.

Pilotage

This is the art of navigating from safe water outside a harbour to your berth, avoiding any dangers en route. This could be navigating into New York Harbor from the Ambrose Lighthouse, or through the Needles Channel at the western entrance of the Isle of Wight from the safe water mark there. Pilotage is also needed in the middle of passages if your route takes you through confined waters, like the Chenal du Four between Ushant and France when heading south to Bordeaux from the UK.

Pilotage is different to offshore passage navigation in that it is very visual, and depends on sailing your vessel along well-defined legs with clear indicators. There is generally no time to go below and plot pilotage on the chart, so you need all the information on deck. It can be quite time-consuming to prepare properly, but is essential for a safe entry into port, especially if conditions are tricky. It is, after all, the shallow bits at the beginning and end of a journey that do the damage – the blue water sections in the middle are generally more straightforward.

Clearing bearings

This is an excellent technique used for **staying to one side of a known danger**. Let's say you're approaching Tor Bay from the north, and want to stop in Torquay alongside the pier to make use of the crane there to do some work on your mast. There are several unmarked rocks and small islands at the NE entrance to the bay. By using two clearing bearings in succession you can stay clear of all of these with a minimum of fuss and a maximum of visual certainty.

To start with you need to avoid Tucker Rock and the Ore Stone. Draw a **clearing bearing** on the very obvious Berry Head lighthouse. By staying to the east, you will be in safe water, clearing the Ore Stone by about 4 cables, or 0.4 nautical miles. By staying east, the bearing of Berry Head will be greater than your clearing bearing. If you are to the west it will be less – and you only need to remember one number!

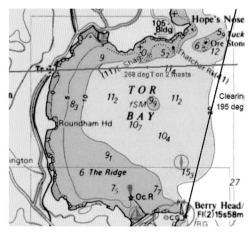
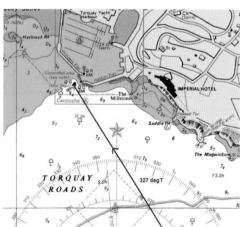

As you pass the Ore Stone, (which at 32m high should be visible even at night), start looking to the west for the two masts, 284m high lit with red lights. Once seen, monitor their bearing until it becomes more than 268°T and head towards them. Just so long as you are south of this line, with the bearing to the masts greater than the clearing bearing of 268°T, you are in safe water to the south of the Ore Stone, Thatcher Rock and East Shag.

Use of depth contours

Depth contours can make excellent clearing lines. As in the previous example, if you stay deeper than the 20m contour while heading south past the Ore Stone, and then deeper than the 10m contour while heading west past the Ore Stone, Thatcher Rock and East Shag, you will be in safe water. It is vital that you **reduce measured depths to soundings,** i.e. take off the tide from your echo sounder reading, for this.

Approaching the port

As you head in, keeping south of the clearing bearing of 268°T on the masts, start to identify features nearer Torquay itself. The steep cliffs and headlands are quite imposing, and there is a rock arch at London Bridge that may be visible. The grand edifice of the Imperial Hotel will be easy to spot, especially at night with all the lights on, and the piers protecting the harbour itself, will become easier to see. The southern pier, Haldon Pier, has a quick green flashing light visible for 6 nautical miles, and just to the west of it is a QG flashing starboard hand marker. When this bears 327°T (or when the pier QG bears 330°T, should the buoy be difficult to see), turn towards it and start your approach. Keep an eye on its bearing, as cross-tide effects may take you one side or another, and warn the crew to keep a good lookout for unlit yellow markers , especially the two closest to the harbour just under half a cable off to port of your ideal track.

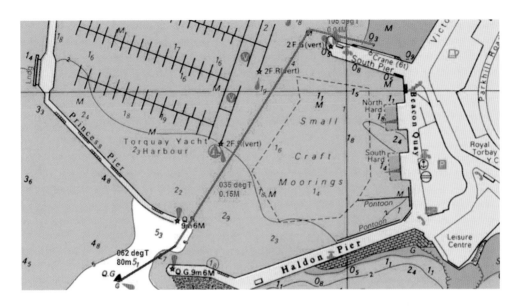

Detailed pilotage plan

This should be made on the most detailed chart you have. The crane is on the north side of South Pier, and the three legs shown will take you there. Each leg of a pilotage plan should have as a minimum fours pieces of information: **starting point, finish point, distance direction.**

The start and finish points should be identifiable by eye or instrument; for example, next to a buoy, between two breakwaters or between a hammerhead pontoon and a pier end. Ideally they should be lit in case you arrive there after dark. The annotated chart (above) has all the information required for a pilotage plan, but a chart can sometimes be unwieldy on deck, especially in heavy weather. Some navigators overcome this by drawing out a separate pilotage plan, but make sure that

you study the chart properly – and replicate the hazards and landmarks correctly, to avoid potential danger and embarrassment.

Draw your track on the chart. Everything you see to port needs to be annotated on the left. Everything to starboard goes on the right. Any leg information goes in the middle.

This **starts** between the pier ends at the harbour entrance, and **finishes** on a line to the Old Fish Quay between the north end of the second hammerhead pontoon and the South Pier. The course is **0.15 nautical miles long on a heading of 035°T.** In addition, you have the first hammerhead coming up on the port side after 0.06 nautical miles, marked by 2 vertical fixed reds, and after another 0.05 miles, the second hammerhead is similarly marked. On the starboard side there are small craft moorings, so keep a lookout for unlit moored yachts or tenders. There is also depth information.

Back bearings

These are very useful for keeping you on a particular bearing from a start point when tide and leeway are taking you sideways.

To make an entry into St Mawes from the flashing green starboard hand marker, you could safely do so by taking a back bearing of 240°T on it.

Keep sighting down the bearing, not directly at the buoy, since this will show you to which side of the track you have drifted. Transits also provide visual pilotage headings and clearing lines.

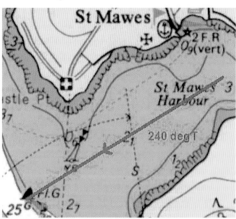

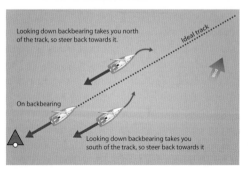

Passage planning and execution

Passage planning looks after the part of the voyage from safe water outside your point of departure to safe water outside your destination.

As the saying goes – 'no battle plan survives contact with the enemy', but with a decent passage plan you can enjoy safe, purposeful cruising and get where you originally set out to go.

There are a few basic concepts to consider:

Waypoints

These are simply points of navigational significance. In general, these are the 'corners' in your route, but you can place them anywhere you like. There is nothing wrong with using buoys as waypoints, but remember to keep a good watch when coming near – yachts have a nasty habit of hitting them when running on autopilot guided by GPS!

Tidal gates

These are areas of tidal concern, such as tidal height constraint when exiting a lock or harbour entrance with a sill across it. A strong tidal flow running against a stiff wind can also cause uncomfortable or potentially dangerous sea states in certain areas.

Alternative ports

These are ports that you can plan to divert to if the weather takes a change of the worse, the vessel suffers mechanical failure or you experience other problems.

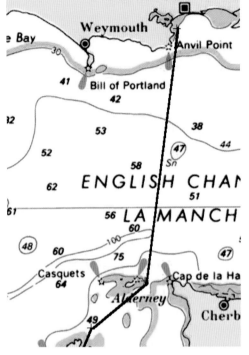

Passage planning example

You are at anchor in Studland Bay off the Dorset coast in England and planning to sail to St Peter Port, on Guernsey in the Channel Islands the next day, Friday, 13 February 2009. The first step is to look at the **overall journey.**

Leg 1: This is 57 miles long, from departure cross Channel from Studland Bay to the centre of the Alderney Race. The leg starts from Waypoint 1, one nautical mile east of Old Harry, a very obvious limestone pillar.

This is a fairly arbitrary choice, and keeps you away from any shallows and overfalls until you are past Anvil Point and in open water.

From there, Leg 1 goes cross-Channel. Running your finger down the track you see there are no fixed dangers – though there will be many ships going up and down the main shipping lanes to watch out for. At the end of Leg 1, there is plenty of space coming through the Alderney Race, just so long as you are on track and have the tide right.

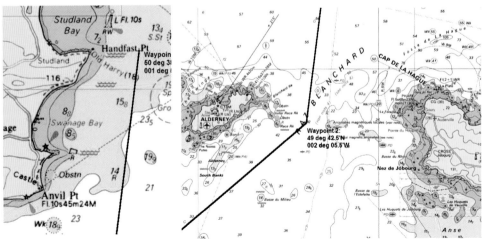

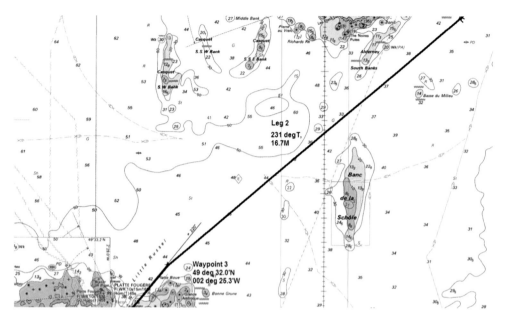

Leg 2
231 degT,
16.7M

Waypoint 3
49 deg 32.0'N
002 deg 25.3'W

Leg 2: From the Alderney race to a waypoint on the leading lights marking the Little Russel channel to St Peter Port.

It is important to draw the track and note its heading and length **on the chart**. By running your finger along the track you check that you are not getting too close to any dangers – such as the Banc de la Schole, which is a safe distance off to the south.

This is the end of the passage plan – from Waypoint 3 to St Peter Port it is now a pilotage plan, and quite a busy and detailed one too.

Timing your passage

So far so good – you know where you're going, and you have the ideal tracks drawn on the charts that you are going to use. So, when to leave, and when to arrive?

This looks fine, though technically speaking the weather may occasionally be a bit rough, but at least it will be a reaching or downwind passage and you will be able to sail your course. Now look at the tides for **potential tidal gates**. There are two in this case:

• The Alderney Race, where tides can reach over 9 knots;

• St Peter Port itself, where the marina entrance has a sill with a drying height of 4.20m.

First, check the weather. The Met Office web site gives the shipping forecast for UK and northern European waters www.metoffice. gov.uk/weather/marine The NOAA site does the same for North American waters www. nws.noaa.gov/om/marine/home.htm The Euroweather site covers the Mediterranean. www.eurometeo.com/english/marine

Of the two, the first is more important. If you get to the marina entrance at the wrong time you can simply tie up to the waiting pontoon and put the kettle on, whereas if you get the tide wrong at the Alderney Race it will be, at best, very uncomfortable and slow, or worse – extremely dangerous.

The tidal stream atlas shows the best time to get there is just before HW Dover, when the tide is slack prior to ebbing, which will then take you all the way down to St Peter Port.

The ideal times to get to the Alderney Race are 1300UT on the 13th or 0100UT on the 14th.

Leg 1 is 57 nautical miles long. At an average of 5 knots, this will take 11 to 12 hours to complete, though it is always a good idea to allow extra time for unforseen circumstances. This would mean weighing anchor at 0000 UT on the 13th. This would have the advantage of an afternoon or early evening entry into St Peter Port, so this is a good option. Leg 2 is 16.7 miles long, and should take about 3 hours with the tide behind you,

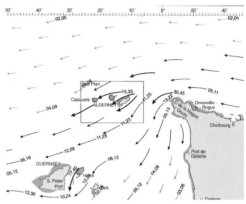

Looking at the tidal data for Dover we have:

Dover, 13th Feb 2009

HW	0112UT	6.9m
LW	0851UT	0.5m
HW	1333UT	6.5m
LW	2103UT	0.9m

14 Feb 2009

HW	0148UT	6.8m
LW	0924UT	0.8m
HW	1409UT	6.3m
LW	2103UT	1.2m

putting you at the entrance to the Little Russel channel at about 1600.

The pilotage is just over 6 miles long, so should take a further hour, and with the sun setting on the 13th at 1726UT, there should be reasonable light for the final part of the voyage.

You need to do a tidal curve for St Peter Port, which in this case, tells you that at 1900UT there is about 6.5m of tide, giving 2.3m over the sill. For most cruising yachts this gives only a small clearance, so you may have to wait until about 1900UT before entering the marina.

Alternative ports

On any passage you should think about the options for stopping off should the weather break or should anyone fall will or hurt themselves.

On this passage, if something were to happen halfway across the Channel, Cherbourg would be the obvious spot – a large port with all-tide, all-weather access. However, as you close on the Alderney Race Cherbourg becomes less attractive, since the adverse tide will be running quite strongly eastwards along the coast. So now, Braye Harbour on Alderney becomes the best option.

This requires a pilotage plan to be made in advance just in case, coupled with a thorough study of the tides around the harbour entrance.

Calculating the overall tidal influence for an individual leg

Calculating a course to steer for a 60 mile leg is a little more involved than doing it for a trip that will only take an hour or so. One way to give yourself a good idea of the overall tidal set and drift is to look at the individual hours on your projected track. A simple table will do:

As this is over 12 hours, an average tidal rate can be calculated:

Average tide =

1.7M/12 hours = 0.15kts to the East.

This can then be put into a standard Course to Steer triangle.

Hour	West Going	East Going
1	0.4	-
2	1.5	-
3	3.0	-
4	3.3	-
5	2.6	-
6	1.9	-
7	0.4	0.8
8	0.4	2.0
9	0.4	3.9
10	0.4	3.9
11	0.4	3.2
12	0.4	0.6
Totals	12.7 M west	14.4 M east
Overall	1.7 M east	-

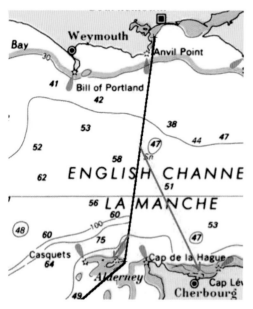

In practice, it is unlikely that this will work out exactly for several reasons, so it is a good idea to re–do your EP whenever the distance to the end of the leg reduces by half: for this passage, after 30 miles, then 45, and then whenever you feel a need to recheck.

What happens over the ground is that you will be taken nearly 13 miles west of your plotted track, and then brought back just over 14 miles by the east-going flood tide. This may look alarming as you plot your hourly positions, but by keeping a good track of where you are in relation to the tide you should see yourself slide back to where you should be.

One way of keeping on top of things is to do a **predictive EP** on every hourly fix. Put your fix on the chart, then do an EP using your average speed and heading, together with whatever the tide is predicted to be for the next hour. In an hour's time, your next fix should be pretty close to the predicted EP. If not, it's a good sign that things are not as they should be.

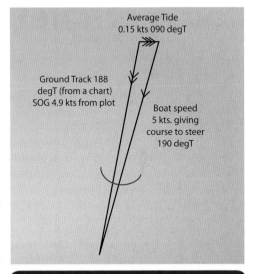

Average Tide
0.15 kts 090 degT

Ground Track 188 degT (from a chart)
SOG 4.9 kts from plot

Boat speed
5 kts. giving
course to steer
190 degT

Navigation tip

SHAPE - a passage
MONITOR - as you go
ADJUST - to the changing conditions

Radio etiquette

Every vessel fitted with a radio transmitter is required to have a Ship Radio Licence, and from this comes the vessel's unique call sign. This is made up of letters and numbers and is spelt out using the phonetic alphabet.

If your vessel has only a hand-held VHF set, a Ship Portable Radio Licence is required. The radio transmitter can only be operated by a ship's radio licence holder with a Short Range Certificate, or crew member under their control.

The latest digital VHF sets operate on the Global Maritime Distress and Safety System (GMDSS). This was introduced to ensure that a vessel can transmit a distress alert automatically. When connected to a GPS receiver, the system will also send your position with a distress alert.

Using a VHF radio

① Press to talk (PTT) microphone. Press the PTT button and the set switches from receive to transmit. Hold the microphone 2inches (5cm) from your mouth and speak slowly and clearly. Say 'Over' at the end of the message and release the PTT button.
② Scan. This allows the set to monitor several channels at one time.

③ DW (Dual Watch). This allows the set to monitor priority channel 16 and one other channel.
④ High/low power. Use low power for all routine calls
⑤ Squelch. A filter to reduce background noise. Adjust knob until interference noise is just audible.

Distress button

This is on VHF-DSC sets only and is protected by a cover. The set has to be programmed with the name and type of the vessel. For a Mayday call, open the cover and press the button. Then press it again for 5 seconds. The alert will then be retransmitted every 4 minutes until a Coastguard station or other vessel responds. The nature of the distress can be defined by scrolling down the menu. NEVER test the DSC by initiating a distress alert.

Phonetic alphabet

Use the phonetic alphabet to spell out yacht names, call signs, abbreviations and words

A	ALPHA	N	NOVEMBER
B	BRAVO	O	OSCAR
C	CHARLIE	P	PAPA
D	DELTA	Q	QUEBEC
E	ECHO	R	ROMEO
F	FOXTROT	S	SIERRA
G	GOLF	T	TANGO
H	HOTEL	U	UNIFORM
I	INDIA	V	VICTOR
J	JULIET	W	WHISKEY
K	KILO	X	X-RAY
L	LIMA	Y	YANKEE
M	MIKE	Z	ZULU

Over: I have finished talking and require an answer.

Out: I have finished talking and do not require an answer. Never finish a conversation with 'Over and Out', as it will lead to much ridicule and cost you a round of drinks.

Say Again: Repeat what you have just said.

Correction: An error has been made; the corrected version is to follow.

I Say Again: I am repeating my previous information.

VHF channel allocation

16: primary distress working channel, and general call-up channel

13: primary inter-bridge channel for matters relating to collision avoidance

06, 08, 72 and 77: main intership channels

70: digital signal for DSC traffic

Testing your VHF

Coastguard stations are quite happy to receive test calls, but do bear in mind that in busy waters, should 324 yachts call in on Channel 16 all requesting a radio check, this important distress channel will become clogged. So, look up the Routine Traffic channel for the Coastguard in the local almanac and make your radio check call on that instead.

Calling other yachts

The VHF radio is a convenient and free means of communication but, as with the radio check calls, you don't want to hog Channel 16 discussing where to have dinner that night. So, when calling up another yacht, once you have made contact on 16, move to an intership channel.

Safety at sea

Plan ahead!

Whenever you go sailing, make sure you have a plan – even if it's just to go from one side of the harbour to the other. On any trip, there are a few basic things that will always be relevant:

- Weather – the forecast should be obtained.
- Tides – these should be checked, and any interaction with strong winds should be noted.
- State of vessel – have you forgotten anything?
- Enough provisions and a little bit more in case things change.
- Do you have enough crew of the right experience levels for your trip?

Register with the Coastguard

By asking for and filling out a CG66 form from the Coastguard, you give all the relevant details of your vessel to them – type, size, colour, sail number, etc. This can be downloaded from www.mcga.gov.uk

File a plan

Before setting out on even a day sail, tell family or friends where you intend to go and when to expect you back. Make sure that they have a note of your mobile/cell phone number and name and the sail number of the yacht.

If you are planning to go offshore, then file your intended route and destination with the Coastguard. In some countries this can be done online, but in others, you can mail a postcard giving all the details of your yacht, including radio call sign and mobile/cell phone number.

HM COASTGUARD SAFETY IDENTIFICATION SCHEME CG66

Traditional passive radar reflector mounted on the mast.

Electronic active radar provides a stronger signal than the passive radar reflector.

Radar reflectors

Always have a radar reflector in the rigging. An aluminium mast does not provide a big enough echo on its own. The International Maritime Organization (IMO) regulations rule that all vessels of 49ft (15m) and above require a reflector with a 10 m^2 echoing area, but these are not always practical to carry in the rigging of smaller yachts. In such cases, the reflector should have the greatest echoing area practical. In all cases, the reflector must be mounted as high as possible for maximum detection range and at a minimum 13ft (3.96m) above sea level.

Electronic radar target enhancers offer another solution and are considered as 'other means' within the Regulations. These have a larger equivalent radar cross section for a physically smaller size and produce an active response on a radar display, which is stronger and more consistent than traditional passive reflectors, without increasing the apparent size of the target.

Man aloft

When hoisting a crew member aloft in a bosun's chair, the halyard must be manned by two crew, one winding the winch, the other tailing and monitoring progress.

- Mast man must be attached to a second halyard for safety and wear a life jacket and safety helmet.
- Tools should be carried in a bag or bucket attached to the bosun's chair.
- The halyard winch must be secured with two tugman's hitches and never left unattended.
- When ascending the mast, the man aloft should assist by pulling himself up the rigging.

- A third crew member can also assist by sweating up the halyard.
- NEVER stand immediately below the man working aloft.
- On descent, the man aloft should slide down the mast, grasping it with arms and legs while the tailer gradually releases the halyard.

Fire – Common causes:
- Smoking below deck
- Gas or gasoline vapour build-up in bilges
- Cooking

Avoidance:
- Never smoke below decks, or while close to sails. Smoking on deck should be at the skipper's discretion.
- Turn the gas tap off whenever the cooker is not in use.
- Keep a fire blanket within reach of the galley. This is best for smothering flames, especially fat fires and clothing that is alight.
- CO_2/halocarbon fire extinguishers are best for use in enclosed spaces.
- Water splashed from a bucket will douse flaming glass-fibre, woodwork and sails.
- The gas bottle must be stowed in a sealed locker that drains overboard. Gas is heavier than air and will sink into the bilges.
- Gasoline (for the outboard engine) should be stowed with the gas bottles in a sealed locker that drains overboard. If the outboard itself is stowed below on larger yachts, it is good practice to disconnect the fuel tank while the engine is running, so that the engine runs dry and does not have any gasoline in its fuel system when stowed.

In the event of gas or gasoline vapour escape:
- Put out cigarettes.
- Open all hatches to vent fresh air through the boat.
- Bail out gas and vapour from the bilge with a bucket.
- Do not turn on or off any electrical systems – the action of opening or closing the switch may cause a spark.

In the event of fire:
- Get everyone on deck and wearing lifejackets.
- Send MAYDAY message and fire distress signals.
- PREPARE TO ABANDON SHIP.

Grab bag
Every yacht should have an emergency grab bag onboard containing critical safety and survival gear such as flares, EPIRB, VHF radio and other personal belongings. Stored in a cockpit locker, it is ready to be grabbed by the crew at a moment's notice and taken onboard the life raft if there is a need to abandon ship.

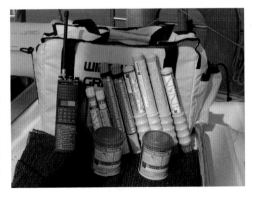

Flares

Flares should be stored in a waterproof container and checked each year to ensure that they are in date. Those that are out of date must be replaced immediately.

Inshore emergency flare pack

for use up to 3 miles from shore.
- 2 red hand -held flares
- 2 orange hand-held smoke flares

Coastal flare pack

for use up to 7 miles offshore.
- 2 red parachute rockets
- 2 red hand-held flares
- 2 orange hand-held smoke flares

Offshore flare pack

For use more than 7 miles offshore.
- 4 red hand flares,
- 2 orange buoyant smokes flares
- 4 red parachute rockets

Offshore flare pack for coastal cruising/racing further than 7 miles offshore.
- 4 red parachute rockets
- 4 red hand-held flares
- 2 orange hand-held smoke flares
- 4 white hand-held collision flares

Emergency Radio Usage

Channel 16 is the Emergency Broadcast Channel and an emergency call is addressed to all stations (other radios) within this transmitting range (approximately 30 miles, 148km, on VHF). When an emergency transmission is made, all other calls on Channel 16 must cease immediately!

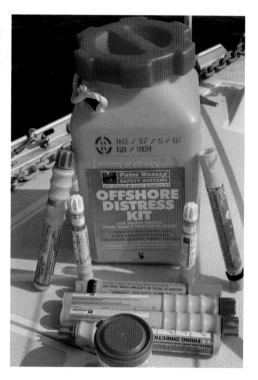

There are three levels of emergency calls.

First Level Emergency: 'MAYDAY - MAYDAY - MAYDAY!'.
- The distress signal is to be used only when there is grave danger to boat or crew.

Second Level Emergency: 'PAN-PAN - PAN-PAN - PAN-PAN!'

This 'urgency' signal should be used when there is a serious, but not life threatening situation that requires assistance including:
- serious illness or injury;
- the skipper is incapacitated;
- you are in danger of being swept ashore by high seas or currents.

Latitude and longitude or

Distance and bearing from a headland or landmark.

- The nature of your problem.
- The number of persons on board and if there are any injuries.
- Description of your boat, including:

  Size

  Colour

  Type of design

  Manufacturer

The latest digital selective calling equipment combines the functionality of voice-only equipment and a distress button, which automatically sends a digital distress signal identifying the calling vessel and the nature of the emergency. When connected to a GPS receiver, the system will also include the vessel's position within the message. While you are calling for help, the crew should be doing what they can to attract attention for help: setting off distress flares in the event of a MAY DAY, or signalling with white flares, raising flags, and waving arms up and down in lesser emergencies. If you cannot see another vessel or land, then use parachute flares.

Other signals for summoning help:

Third Level Emergency:

'SECURITE - SECURITE - SECURITE!'

This signal is used to warn of conditions that may affect other sailors in the area, including:

- hazards to navigation such as drifting containers, logs, nets, etc;
- warnings from large vessels entering a narrow channel;
- you have broken down or run out of fuel;
- you have a rope round your prop;

The emergency rescue service then needs:

- Your vessel's name, repeated 3 times.
- The position of your boat, either:

LIFE SAVING SIGNALS

To be used by Ships, Aircraft or Persons in Distress, when c
rescue operations.

Search and Rescue Unit Replies

You have been seen, assistance will be given as soon as possible.

Orange smoke flare

Three white star signals or three light and sound rockets fired at
approximately 1 minute intervals.

Air to Surface Direction Signals

Your assistance is no
longer required.

Sequence of 3 manoeuvres meaning proceed to this direction.

Cross low, astern
of vessel, rocking wings.

Circle vessel at
least once.

Cross low, ahead of a vessel
rocking wings.

Overfly vessel and head
in required direction.

Shore to Ship Signals

Safe to land here.

Landing here is dangerous. Additional signals mean safer
landing in direction indicated.

Vertical waving of both arms,
white flag, light or flare.

Horizontal waving of white flag, light or flare. Putting one flag,
light or flare on ground and moving off with a second indicates
direction of safer landing.

K: ▬ ● ▬
Morse code signal
by light or sound.

S: ● ● ●
Morse code
signals by light
or sound.

R: ● ▬ ●
Land to the right
of your current
heading.

L: ● ▬ ● ●
Land to the left
of your current
heading.

...unicating with life saving stations, maritime rescue units and aircraft engaged in search and

Surface to Air Signals

Note: Use International Code of Signals by means of lights or flags or by laying out the symbol on the deck or ground with items which have a high contrast to the background.

Message	ICAO/IMO Visual Signals
Require assistance	V
Require medical assistance	X
No or negative	N
Yes or affirmative	Y
Proceeding in this direction	

Air to Surface Replies

Message Understood.

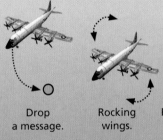

Drop a message.

Rocking wings.

Flashing landing or navigation lights on and off twice

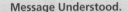
T: ▬▬▬   R: ●▬▬●
Morse code signal by light.

Message Not Understood – Repeat.

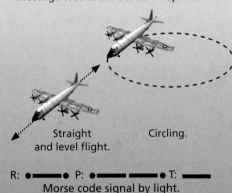

Straight and level flight.

Circling.

R: ●▬▬● P: ●▬▬▬▬● T: ▬▬
Morse code signal by light.

Surface to Air Replies

Message Understood – I will comply.

T: ▬▬
Morse code signal by light.

Code & answering pendant 'Close Up'.

Change course to required direction.

I am unable to comply.

Note: Use the signal most appropriate to prevailing conditions.

T: ▬▬
Morse code signal by light.

International flag 'N'.

Man overboard

This is every sailor's worst nightmare, and prevention is definitely better than cure. Being physically attached to the boat is an excellent first step, and so your lifelines should be used whenever there is any danger of unsteady motion on the boat. Remember that if you go overboard at night or in bad weather there is a significant risk that you will not be found, so practise man overboard drills regularly, and CLIP ON. The fundamental components to the drill are:

STOP THE BOAT – RAISE THE ALERT – LOCATE THE CASUALTY

If someone goes overboard, follow this standard procedure:

- Raise the alarm by **shouting** 'MAN OVERBOARD'.
- Keep at least one person **looking and pointing** at the casualty. This person is VITAL, and should not do anything else.
- **Throw** the danbuoy and two horseshoe floats immediately.

Man overboard recovery using engine

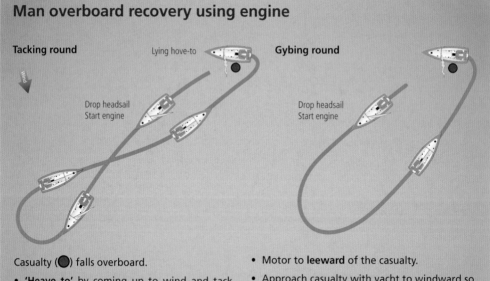

Tacking round Lying hove-to **Gybing round**

Wind

Drop headsail
Start engine

Drop headsail
Start engine

Casualty (●) falls overboard.

- **'Heave to'** by coming up to wind and tack, leaving the headsail backed and hauling mainsheet in as close as possible.
- **Throw** the marker devices as soon as possible.
- At the same time, **start the engine** (checking that no lines are over the side).
- **Drop the headsail** and staysail.

- Motor to **leeward** of the casualty.
- Approach casualty with yacht to windward so that it is blown down on to the casualty when it stops, not blown further away.
- Depower the mainsail by releasing the vang and sheeting out till it flaps. It is important that the rescuing party remains forward of the shrouds so as not to be injured by the boom.

Man overboard recovery under sail

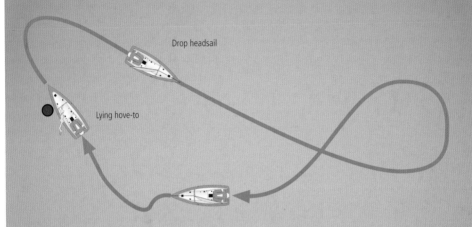

Drop headsail

Lying hove-to

Casualty (●) falls overboard.

- 'Heave to' by coming up to wind and tack, leaving the headsail backed and hauling mainsheet in as close as possible.

- Throw the marker devices overboard as soon as possible.

- Put the boat on beam reach, and if the wind is sufficient to maintain way under main alone, drop the headsails.

- Allow yourself sea room to manoeuvre and tack, but don't let the casualty go out of sight.

- Sail far enough downwind so that when you go up to the casualty you are sailing on a fine reach. This will allow you to maintain

control, but also to depower the mainsail easily to stop.

- Point directly at the casualty. If the main can be depowered completely by dumping the mainsheet, then the boat can be stopped. If not, duck sharply downwind for 3 boat lengths and point again at the casualty to see if the main can be depowered. Once it can, then the ideal fine reach approach can be started.

- Approach casualty on a fine reach, easing the sheet in the final stages. Leeway will increase as you slow down.

- Recover the casualty on leeward side of the yacht.

MOB recovery procedure when flying a spinnaker

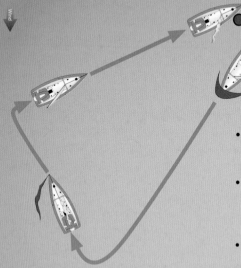

Casualty (⬤) falls overboard.

- Throw in the marker devices as soon as possible.

- Assign one, or preferably two people to watch the casualty. At this point the yacht will be going away from the casualty at up to half a mile every 2 minutes, so speed of reaction is of the utmost importance. Come up to the wind, but DO NOT TACK.

- As the yacht comes up to the wind, the working guy is run. The pole will hit the forestay, so the guy should be let out in a controlled manner until this happens, after which it can be released.

- Lazy spinnaker sheet MUST be free to run. Allows the spinnaker to flap behind the mainsail, which will also be depowered as the yacht comes toward the wind.

- The guy and the lazy spinnaker sheet will run out rapidly, so ensure that no-one's foot is trapped in a loop of line.

- The yacht will now be virtually stopped, with the spinnaker flapping very noisily, the people pointing at the casualty must maintain concentration.

- Recover the spinnaker through the letter box by pulling in on the lazy guy, leaving the yacht with just the mainsail hoisted.

- If conditions do not allow the above procedure, then simply release the spinnaker halyard, then the guy and sheet and let the spinnaker and its associated lines fall away. The loss of a sail is insignificant when compared to the loss of a person.

- The mainsail is controlled as required by the mainsheet.

- Check for lines in the water.

- Start the engine.

- The boat is tacked.

- Approach the casualty on a fine reach and pick up on the leeward side, depowering the mainsail at the final stage. Refer back to the 'Using Engine' section for this.

- Press the 'MOB' and then 'ENTER' buttons on the GPS, check there are no lines over the side and start the engine.
- Start recovery manoeuvre (see following sections).
- In darkness use searchlight to illuminate search area
- Send MAYDAY call on the VHF or satellite phone.
- Assume in temperate climate zones that the casualty will be suffering from hypothermia and prepare for this.

What to do if you are overboard

- To quote the well-known book – STAY CALM. Panic will kill you long before the sea does.
- Inflate your life jacket.
- Turn your light on by pulling the toggle.
- Pull the spray hood over your head if spray is making it difficult to breath.
- Locate the yacht, but do not swim towards it
- Locate any emergency equipment, e.g. the danbuoy or a horseshoe, which has been thrown from the yacht, and if possible swim towards that.
- Use your whistle to make sound signals, it is the best value for money piece of lifesaving equipment you have. The sound is far easier to hear than shouting, and much less effort to produce.
- Do not expend energy.
- Cross your arms over your chest under your life jacket to keep as much warmth in you as possible.

Recovering an Unconscious Casualty from the Water

- There are various recovery methods from deploying a life sling to using a sail as a cradle to hoist the casualty back onboard using a mast halyard. If your yacht has a transom step, then encourage the swimmer to reach the stern and pull them up over the step. Whichever system you adopt, practise it beforehand and make sure it works on your yacht.
- Sending the bowman overboard to assist the casualty should always be the last resort. The last thing you want is to have two casualties in the water!
- Ensure that the casualty is lifted back onboard as close to a horizontal posture as possible.

Practice can save lives – perhaps your own!

If you are planning a passage offshore, then the crew should be fully briefed about man overboard routines as part of the safety briefing. The routine can then be put into practice by dropping a fender over the side without warning as if it was the skipper, who should then withdraw to monitor progress as the crew learn to retrieve it.

Glossary of terms

ABACK – When the headsail is sheeted to the windward side and the yacht is hove-to.

ABAFT – Behind or towards the stern.

ABEAM – At right angles to the boat.

ADMIRALTY STOPPER KNOT – A permanent stopper knot.

AFT – See Abaft.

AIRFLOW – Flow of air across the sails.

ALTO – Middle-level cloud base.

ALTOCUMULUS – Middle-level cloud.

ALTOSTRATUS – Middle-level cloud.

AMIDSHIPS – Centre of the boat.

ABOUT – To go about is to tack the yacht through the wind.

ANCHOR – Device to moor the yacht in open water on the end of a line.

ANEMOMETER – Instrument to measure wind speed.

ANTICYCLONE – Meteorological term describing area of high pressure.

APPARENT WIND – The wind experienced by a moving boat. If the boat is stationary, the apparent wind is the same as the true wind. If the boat is moving towards the wind, the apparent wind is greater than the true wind. If the boat is moving away from the wind, the apparent wind is less than the true wind.

ASPECT RATIO – The aspect ratio of a sail is its width measured against its depth of curvature, or height compared to its width. Hence, a high aspect ratio mainsail refers to a tall narrow shape.

ASYMMETRIC SPINNAKER – Downwind sail with a fixed luff, which is tacked or gybed like a jib.

ATHWARTSHIPS – From one side of the vessel to the other.

BACKING THE JIB – Setting the jib on the weather side to encourage the boat to bear away.

BACKWIND – When the airflow across the jib causes the mainsail to flutter.

BAILER – Scoop to remove water from inside the boat.

BALANCE – Reference to relative balance between the hydrostatic lift on the hull and the central point of the rig. This is measured by the degree of weight or pressure on the tiller, giving weather helm when too heavy and boat wants to point up, and lee helm when too light and boat wants to bear away.

BATTEN – Flexible strip of wood or reinforced resin to stiffen the leech of the sail.

BEAM – Mid part of the boat, or measurement of maximum width of the hull.

BEAM REACH – Sailing with the wind directly abeam.

BEAR AWAY – To turn the bows away from the wind.

BEARING – Compass direction.

BEAT – The close-hauled, zigzag course to windward.

BEATING – Sailing close-hauled to windward.

BEAUFORT SCALE – Scale of wind speeds devised by Admiral Sir Francis Beaufort.

BECKET – A second eye or attachment point in a pulley block.

BERMUDA RIG – Single masted sail plan with tall, triangular mainsail.

BIGHT – An open loop in a rope.

BLACK BANDS – Narrow bands painted on the mast and boom to mark the maximum extension of the mainsail luff and foot.

BLOCK – A pulley.

BLOCK AND TACKLE – A multi-purchase pulley system.

BOLT ROPE – Rope sewn or enclosed in the luff of the mainsail.

BOOM – Spar attached to the foot of the mainsail – and sometimes the jib.

BOOM VANG – Multi-purchase system or lever, also known as a kicking strap, to prevent the boom from rising and to control the shape of the mainsail.

BOTTLE SCREW – Screw system used to tension rigging.

BOW – Front end of the boat.

BOWLINE – A knot used to tie a loop into the end of a rope.

BOWSPRIT – Spar that extends forward of the bow to support an asymmetric spinnaker.

BREAKWATER – Small upstanding ledge or coaming across the foredeck to deflect water.

BROACH – When a yacht slews out of control broadside to the wind and sea.

BROAD REACH – Point of sail when wind is abaft the beam.

BULLSEYE – Wooden block or thimble with a hole drilled through it to take a rope to act as a block or stopper.

BULKHEAD – Transverse partition within the boat.

BUNG – Plug to block a drainage hole.

BUOY – Floating racing mark or navigation mark.

BUOYANCY – Power to float, having a density less than water.

BUOYANCY BAGS/TANKS – Built-in buoyancy to support the boat in the event of a capsize.

BURGEE – Small flag flown from the masthead.

BUTTHOIST – The car to which the butts (mast end) of the spinnaker poles are fixed when in use.

CAM CLEAT – Cleat with two spring-load cams to hold a rope.

CAMBER – Curvature of a sail.

CAPSIZE – Point when the mast of a sailboat touches the water.

CATAMARAN – Twin-hulled vessel.

CENTRE OF BUOYANCY – Point where the buoyant force of water acts on the hull.

CENTRE OF EFFORT – Point where the force of wind acts on the rig.

CENTRE OF PRESSURE – Point where the side force of wind acts on the hull.

CENTREBOARD – Retractable keel that limits leeway, or the sideways force of the sails.

CHAIN PLATE – Hull or deck fitting to which the shroud is attached.

CHART – Map of the sea.

CHINE – Line or crease in the hull. A hull built from flat sheets of plywood is known as a hard chine boat.

CHINESE GYBE – Involuntary crash gybe.

CHORD DEPTH – Maximum depth of an aerofoil section.

CIRRUS – High-level cloud.

CIRROCUMULUS – High-level cloud.

CIRROSTRATUS – High-level cloud with little form.

CLAM CLEAT – Cleat with no moving parts that secures rope within its grooved, V-shaped body.

CLEAR ASTERN / CLEAR AHEAD – One boat is clear astern of another when her hull and equipment in normal position are behind a line abeam from the after most point of the other boat's hull and equipment in normal position. The other boat is clear ahead.

CLEAT – Fitting designed to hold a rope under tension without the use of a knot or hitch.

CLEVIS PIN – Pin that closes the fork of a rigging screw.

CLEW – Lower, aft corner of a sail.

CLEW OUTHAUL – Adjustor to change tension on the clew, and shape of the sail.

CLINKER CONSTRUCTION – Traditional form of hull construction where the planks overlap each other.

CLOSE REACH – Point of sailing midway between close-hauled and a beam reach.

CLOSE-HAULED – Point of sailing closest to wind.

CLOVE HITCH – Common knot or hitch used to tie a rope to a ring or rail.

COAMING – Small upstanding ledge or breakwater across or around the deck to deflect water.

COCKPIT – Area of the yacht where helm and crew operate the boat.

COMPASS – Navigation instrument that points to the magnetic north pole.

CRINGLE – Metal eye or attachment point in each corner of the sail.

CUMULUS – Low-level cloud.

CUMULONIMBUS – Low-level rain cloud.

CUNNINGHAM HOLE – Cringle in luff to attach a purchase to flatten the sail.

CURRENT – A stream of water.

DACRON – American name for man-made sail material named polyester in Europe.

DAGGER BOARD – A vertically retracting keel that limits leeway, or the sideways force of the sails.

DEAD RUN – Sailing dead downwind.

DEPRESSION – Meteorological term for an area of low pressure.

DEVIATION – Compass error influenced by magnetic materials nearby.

DINGHY – Small open boat without a fixed keel.

DIRTY WIND – Disturbed wind or wind shadow effect from another sailboat to windward.

DISPLACEMENT – Volume/weight that a hull displaces in water.

DOWNHAUL – Rope or purchase used to tension the tack of a sail or Cunningham.

DOWNWIND – Sailing in the same direction as the wind.

EASE – To slacken a rope or let a sheet out.

EBB – Outgoing tide or flow.

EDDIES – Area of reverse or back-running current.

FAIRLEAD – A fixed lead to guide a rope or sheet and prevent chafe.

FAIRWAY – Main navigable channel.

FAIR WIND – Wind direction that allows a boat to sail from A to B without tacking.

FATHOM – Nautical unit of measure equal to 6ft (1.828m).

FENDER – Portable cushion or inflatable bladder to protect the hull from rubbing against another boat or a pontoon.

FETCH – Straight course sailed to windward without tacking.

FIGURE-OF-EIGHT KNOT – Stopper knot.

FLOOD TIDE – A rising tide.

FOILS – Collective term for keel, centreboard/dagger board and rudder.

FOLLOWING WIND – Opposite of headwind, when the wind comes from astern.

FORESAIL – Jib or headstay.

FORESTAY – Forward stay supporting the mast.

FOTHERING – The process of stuffing anything that comes to hand (e.g. sleeping bags) into a hole in the boat to stop water ingress.

FREEBOARD – Height of a boat's side above the water.

FRONT – Meteorological term describing a distinct line of weather – cold front, warm front, etc.

FURL – To gather up or reef a sail in an orderly manner.

GAFF – Spar supporting the top of a traditional four-sided mainsail – gaff rig.

GATE START – Method of starting a race with fleet passing behind the stern of a guard boat tracking behind a yacht sailing close-hauled on port tack.

GEL COAT – The smooth waterproof outer resin coating of a fibre-reinforced moulded hull and deck.

GENOA – Large headsail that overlaps the mainsail.

GO ABOUT – To tack through the eye of the wind.

GOOSENECK – Double-hinged fitting to attach boom to mast.

GOOSE-WINGED – Running before the wind with mainsail set on one side and jib 'goose-winged' out on the other.

GPS – Satellite-based global positioning system.

GRADIENT WIND – Meteorological term caused by changes in barometric pressure. The greater the change in pressure, the steeper the gradient.

GRP – Glass reinforced plastic.

GUDGEON – Female part of a pair of rudder hangings into which the male pintle fits.

GUNTER RIG – Traditional high-aspect mainsail with gaff that extends almost vertically up from the mast.

GUNWALE – Outer strengthening piece around the top of the hull.

GUY – Windward spinnaker sheet or boom restrainer.

GYBE – Controlled form of tacking downwind when the transom passes through the eye of the wind and the boom flies across from one side to the other.

HALF HITCH – Temporary knot to attach a rope to a rail.

HALYARD – Rope or wire line to hoist sails up the mast.

HANK – Clip to attach luff or sail to a stay.

HARD CHINE – Line where the flat sheets used to construct a hull meet.

HARDEN UP – To point closer to wind.

HEAD – Top corner of a sail.

HEADBOARD – Reinforced top corner of a mainsail.

HEADING – Direction that a boat is taking.

HEADSAIL – Jib or genoa.

HEADSTAY – Forward stay supporting the mast.

HEAD TO WIND – Boat facing directly into wind – the no-go zone.

HEAD UP – Sailing closer to the wind.

HEAVE TO – To bring the boat to a halt, head to wind, by backing the jib, putting the rudder down and letting the mainsail fly.

HEEL – Bottom end of the mast. The sideways tilt of a sailing boat.

HELM – Rudder. Also short for helmsman or helmsperson.

HIGHFIELD LEVER – A locking lever to tension stays.

HIKE – To sit out and counter the heeling force of the wind.

HITCH – Type of knot for attaching a rope to a rail or hoop.

HOIST – Vertical dimension of a sail or flag.

HOUNDS – Where the shrouds connect to the mast.

HOVE TO – See Heave to.

IMMINENT – Meteorological term for change in weather within six hours.

INGLEFIELD CLIPS – Interlocking C-shaped clips used to attach signal flaps, and sometimes a spinnaker, to a halyard.

IN IRONS – Term used when a sailboat is caught head to wind within the no-go zone.

ISOBAR – Meteorological term for line on weather map linking points of equal atmospheric pressure.

JACKSTAY – A strong webbing strap running the length of the boat on each side. By clipping the lifeline to this, it ensures that Jack stays on the boat.

JIB – Small headsail.

JIB SHEETS – Ropes controlling the set of the jib.

JIB STICK – Pole to goose-wing the jib from when sailing dead downwind. Also known as a whisker pole.

JOCKEY POLE – Short pole used to hold the spinnaker guy away from the stanchions, and to give a better mechanical angle to the guy to hold the spinnaker pole off the forestay when it is far forward.

JUMPER STAY – Stay on the foreside of the mast to prevent the spar from bending forward.

KEDGE – Light, temporary anchor to hold the boat against an adverse tidal stream.

KICKING STRAP – Multi-purchase system or lever, also known as a vang, to prevent the boom from rising and control the shape of the mainsail.

KITE – Abbreviation for spinnaker.

KNOT – Nautical mile per hour (1 nautical mile equals 1.15 statute miles or 1,852m). Also refers to a rope tie.

KNUCKLE – Sharp longitudinal line of distortion within the hull.

LAND BREEZE – Offshore wind, opposite to a sea breeze, that develops when the temperature of the sea is higher than the land.

LANYARD – Short length of cord used as a safety line.

LATERAL RESISTANCE – Ability of a boat to resist leeway or sideways force of the wind.

LAY LINE – The course on which your boat, sailing close-hauled on starboard tack, can just make a windward mark, which is to be rounded to port, is the starboard-tack lay line for that mark. The most windward line on which you would approach the mark on port tack is the port-tack lay line.

LEAD – The direction that a rope is led.

LEE – Opposite to windward. The side away from the wind.

LEECH – Trailing edge of a sail.

LEE BOW – Sailing on a tack where the tidal stream carries the boat towards the wind.

LEE HELM – A sailing boat, which requires its tiller to be pushed down to the leeward side to counter the boat's natural tendency to bear away, is said to carry 'lee helm'. This condition signifies that the rig is out of balance with the hull.

LEE HO – Final warning call of helm as the tiller is pushed over to leeward during a tack.

LEE SHORE – Shoreline which the wind is blowing towards.

LEEWARD – Opposite of windward; away from the wind.

LIFE JACKET – Buoyancy vest designed to keep a nonswimmer or unconscious person floating head up.

LIFT – A shift in the wind that swings aft. Otherwise known as a freeing wind.

LOA – Length overall.

LETTER BOX – The gap between the foot of the mainsail and the boom.

LOOSE-FOOTED – Sail attached to a boom only by the clew and outhaul.

LUFF – The leading edge of a sail.

LUFFING – When a sailboat is steered closer to the wind.

LUFF ROPE – Rope sewn or enclosed in the luff of the mainsail. Also known as bolt rope.

LWL – Load waterline or length of waterline.

 M

MAGNETIC NORTH – Compass heading.

MAGNETIC VARIATION – Difference in angle between True North and Magnetic North.

MAINSAIL – Principal sail set on a mast.

MAINSHEET – Rope attached to the boom to trim the mainsail.

MAMMA – Dark low-level rain cloud with udder-like shape.

MARK – An object (buoy) the sailing instructions require a boat to pass on a specified side.

MAST – A spar going straight up from the deck, used to attach sail and boom.

MARLING HITCH – Line of linked knots tying sail to a spar.

MILLIBAR – Meteorological term for unit of pressure equal to 1/10000th of a bar.

MOULD – Male or female pattern for producing a plastic hull and other mouldings.

MULTIHULL – Generic term for a catamaran or trimaran.

MYLAR – Polyester film used in the manufacture of sails.

 N

NAUTICAL MILE – 1 nautical mile equals 1.15 statute miles or 1,852m.

NEAP TIDES – Tides with the smallest rise and fall. Opposite of spring tides.

NIMBO – Rain cloud.

NIMBOSTRATUS – Middle-level rain cloud.

NO-GO ZONE – Area 40° either side of the direction of the wind.

 O

OBSTRUCTION – An object that a boat cannot pass without changing course substantially to avoid it, e.g. the shore, perceived underwater dangers or shallows.

OCCLUDED FRONT – Meteorological term to describe when a cold front overtakes a warm front.

OFFSHORE WIND – Wind blowing seaward off the land.

OFF WIND – Sailing in the same direction as the wind.

OFF THE WIND – Sailing a course lower than a beam reach.

ONSHORE WIND – Wind blowing inland off the sea.

ON THE WIND – Sailing a close-hauled course.

OOD – Officer of the Day.

OUTHAUL – Line used to stretch the clew of a sail to the end of the boom.

 P

PAINTER – Mooring line.

PELICAN HOOK – Metal hook with a cam-action lock.

PFD – Personal flotation device such as a buoyancy aid or life jacket.

PINCH – Sailing so close to the wind that the sails start to luff and lose drive.

PINTLE – Male part of a pair of rudder hangings that fits into the female gudgeon.

PITCH POLE – When a boat capsizes end over end.

PLANING – When a boat lifts its bows out of the water, and because of the reduced drag, then accelerates onto a planing attitude.

POLED OUT – Running before the wind with mainsail set on one side and the jib poled out or 'goose-winged' on the other.

POINTS OF SAILING – Beating, reaching and running before the wind.

PORT – Left hand side of a boat.

PORT GYBE – Sailing downwind with the wind on the port side of the boat and mainsail out to port. This is the give-way gybe.

PORT TACK – Sailing with the wind on the port (left) side of the boat. This is the give-way tack.

PORTSMOUTH YARDSTICK – Simple sailboat handicapping system when mixed classes race together.

PRE-BEND – Amount of fore and aft bend set in a mast.

PREVENTER – Safety line.

PURCHASE – Mechanical advantage of the block and tackle or lever.

QUARTER – Sides of the boat aft, i.e. starboard quarter, port quarter.

RACE – Fast running tide or stream.

RACING FLAG/PENNANT – Small rectangular flag flown at the masthead to signal that the boat is racing.

RAKE – Degree that a mast leans back from vertical.

RATCHET BLOCK – Purchase block with an integral ratchet to lessen the load of a sheet held in the hand.

REACH – Sailing course with the wind abeam.

REACHING – Sailing with the wind abeam.

REACHING HOOK – Device set close to the shrouds to run the windward spinnaker sheet or guy through.

READY ABOUT – First warning call to the crew that the helm intends to tack.

REEF – To reduce or shorten sail.

REEF KNOT – Knot joining two ropes together.

REEFING – Reducing the amount of sail area.

RHUMB LINE – Straight line between two points drawn on a Mercator chart.

RIDING TURN – When a rope or sheet crosses under itself and jams, most often around a winch.

RIG – General term for mast, spars and sails.

RIGGING – Standing wires that hold up the mast.

RIGGING SCREW – Screw to tension shrouds. Also known as a bottle screw.

RIGHT OF WAY – Term within Collision Regulations denoting a boat with rights, as opposed to a boat that must give way.

ROACH – The top curve within the leech of a mainsail.

ROCKER – Fore and aft curve within the central underside sections of the boat.

ROLL TACKING – Use of crew weight to speed the process of tacking to windward.

ROLLER JIB – Furling headsail.

ROTATING MAST – Spar designed to rotate from port to starboard to present its best aspect to the wind.

ROUND TURN AND TWO HALF HITCHES – Knot used to attach rope to a rail or hoop.

RUBBING STRAKE – A strengthening strip secured to the gunwale as a protective buffer.

RUDDER – Moving foil to steer the boat with.

RUN – Sailing dead downwind.

RUNNING – Sailing before the wind with the sail out.

RUNNING BY THE LEE – Sailing downwind with the mainsail set on the windward side and about to gybe.

RUNNING RIGGING – Sheets and halyards used to set and control the sails.

SAIL TRIM – The position of the sails relative to the wind and desired point of sail. Sails that are not trimmed properly may not operate efficiently. Visible signs of trim are luffing, excessive heeling, and the flow of air past telltales. Also see sail shape.

SEA BREEZE –- Onshore wind opposite to a land breeze, that develops when the temperature of the land is higher than the sea.

SELF BAILER – Thru-hull bailer that, once activated, allows the bilge water to flow out when the keel boat is planing.

SEACOCK – A valve going through the hull, which can be shut from inside the boat.

SEXTANT – A navigational instrument used to determine the vertical position of an object such as the sun, moon or stars. Used with celestial navigation.

SHACKLE – Metal link with screw pin to connect wires and lines.

SHEAVE – The wheel within a block.

SHEEPSHANK – Knot used to shorten a rope.

SHEET – Any rope used to adjust sail shape.

SHEET BEND – Knot used to join two dissimilar sized ropes together.

SHOCK CORD – Elastic or bungee cord made of rubber strands.

SHROUDS – Wires supporting either side of the mast.

SLAB REEF – Method of reefing the mainsail.

SLIP HITCH – A temporary knot used to secure sails.

SLIP LINE – Temporary double line with both ends made fast to the boat that can be released from onboard and pulled in.

SLOT EFFECT – The effect a jib has in accelerating the flow of air around the back of a mainsail.

SNAP SHACKLE – Shackle with a secure locking mechanism instead of a pin.

SPAR – General term for a mast, boom, gaff or spinnaker pole.

SPIGOT – The male prong onto which the female mast end of the spinnaker or jockey pole fits.

SPINNAKER – Large parachute-like downwind sail.

SPINNAKER CHUTE – Open-mouthed tubular container fitted in the bow from which to launch and recover the spinnaker.

SPINNAKER POLE – Spar to set the spinnaker from.

SPREADER – A strut usually fitted in pairs to deflect the shrouds and control the bending characteristics of the mast.

SPRING TIDE – Extreme high tide caused by the gravitational pull of the moon.

STAND-ON-BOAT – Right of way boat.

SQUALL – Sudden, short-lived increase in wind.

STARBOARD – Right hand side of the boat.

STARBOARD GYBE – Sailing downwind with the wind on the starboard side of the boat and mainsail out to port. This is the right-of-way gybe.

STARBOARD TACK – Sailing upwind with the wind on the starboard side of the boat and mainsail out to port. This is the right-of-way tack.

STAY – Forward mast support.

STEM – Forward extremity of the boat.

STERN – Aft extremity of the boat.

STOPPER – A cleating device that holds a sheet or halyard fast.

STRATUS – Featureless low-level cloud.

STRATOCUMULUS – Low-level cloud.

STROP – A ring of rope or wire used to make up an attachment to a spar.

SWIVEL – Connector whose two parts rotate.

SWIVEL BLOCK – Block with a swivel joint.

TABERNACLE – Structure supporting a deck-stepped mast.

TACK – Lower forward corner of a sail.

TACKING – To sail close-hauled through the eye of the wind.

TACKLE – Multi-purchase system.

TAIL – The free end of a sheet or halyard.

TALURIT – Swaged wire splice.

TELLTALES – Strips of fabric or wool attached to the luff of a jib and leech of the mainsail to indicate airflow across the sail.

THWART – Transverse seat or plank amidships.

TIDAL STREAM – Flow of water caused by the rise and fall of tide.

TIDE – Six-hourly rise and fall of water caused by the gravitational pull of the moon.

TILLER – Arm of a rudder to control boat direction.

TILLER EXTENSION – Lightweight pole with universal joint attached to the end of the tiller to allow the helm to sit outboard or steer from the trapeze.

TOE STRAPS – Lengths of webbing running fore and aft in a sailboat for crew to hook their feet under and hike out.

TRAILING EDGE – Aft edge of a foil, i.e. sail, keel, rudder etc.

TRAINING RUN – Sailing downwind 5-10° shy of the dead downwind angle.

TRAMPOLINE – Rope netting or webbing strung between two hulls of a catamaran.

TRANSIT – Sighting two objects in line.

TRANSOM – Transverse aft end of a boat.

TRAPEZE – Harness attached by wire to the hounds of the mast to allow the crew to extend their whole body outboard of the sailboat to improve their righting moment.

TRAVELLER – Fitting on a rope or track with limited travel used to adjust the mainsheet.

TRIM – To adjust the sails to suit the wind direction.

TRIMARAN – Three-hulled multihull.

TRUCKER'S HITCH – Knot used to tension a tie rope.

TRUE WIND – Direction and velocity of wind measured at a stationary position.

TUGMAN'S HITCH – Knot to secure towing strop to winch.

TWIST – Difference in angle to the wind between the top and bottom of a sail.

UNIVERSAL JOINT – Hinge that allows universal movement.

UNSTAYED MAST – Mast without standing rigging.

UPHAUL – Control line to adjust the height of the spinnaker pole.

UPWIND – Any course closer to the wind than a beam reach.

VANG – Multi-purchase system or lever, also known as a kicking strap, to prevent the boom from rising and control the shape of the mainsail.

VARIATION – Difference in angle between True North and Magnetic North.

VMG – Velocity made good to windward.

WAKE – Turbulence left astern of a moving boat.

WARP – Rope used to moor a boat.

WEATHER HELM – A sailing boat, which requires its tiller to be held up towards the weather side to counter the boat's natural tendency to luff, is said to carry 'weather helm'. This condition signifies that the rig is out of balance with the hull.

WEATHER SHORE – Shoreline where the wind is blowing offshore.

WETTED SURFACE – Total underwater area of the hull.

WHISKER POLE – Pole to goose-wing the jib from when sailing dead downwind. Also known as a jib stick.

WINCH – Capstan used to tension sail sheets and halyards.

WINDAGE – Drag caused by the boat and crew.

WINDWARD – Towards the wind; opposite of leeward.

WIND GRADIENT – Difference in wind speed close to the water and a certain height above it such as the masthead. This is not the same as gradient wind, which refers to changes in barometric pressure.

WINDLASS – See *Winch*.

WORKING END – End of a rope used to tie a knot.

Acknowledgements

Our thanks to UKSA who have assisted with the production of this book, in particular, Jon Ely and Simon Rowell whose advice and contributions have been invaluable. They have answered questions, shaped the chapters and been a sounding board on many areas. A charity based in Cowes, UKSA is dedicated to changing lives through maritime activity, and trains almost 7,500 people every year from all backgrounds and to all levels. From children as young as 8 years old learning watersports skills, to the full range of RYA qualifications, and up to MCA Master 3000gt, UKSA is an expert in the watersports and yacht training industry. (*www.uksa.org*).

We must also thank Ian Mills and his team at Performance Laser and designer Tony Castro for allowing the use of the Laser SB3 open keelboat, and to Northshore Yachts, builders of the Southerly swing keel range of cruising yachts to provide realism to the illustrations. A special thanks also goes to illustrator Greg Filip who worked so hard to faithfully reproduce the methodology taught by the UKSA.

David Houghton, the former weather guru to Britain's Olympic sailing team and author of *Weather at Sea* also provided valued advice.

Grateful thanks also go to Roland Eno and the picture research team at PPL Photo Agency, for sourcing the many photographs we required to illustrate particular points throughout the book. We are also grateful to Force 4 Chandlery for loaning equipment we needed to photograph, to Spinlock for allowing us to use and demonstrate their Spinlock Deckvest and safety harness, Seldén Mast AB for use of their headsail furling illustrations, and to Marlow Ropes for providing the cordage used in the knots, ropes and running rigging chapter.

Credits:
All illustrations: *Greg Filip/PPL* Photo Research: *PPL Photo Agency*. Photographs: Alberto Mariotti/PPL: 117. Ancasta Yachts: 17. Barry Pickthall/PPL: 18, 37, 38, 39, 40, 41, 42, 43, 44, 45, 46, 47, 48, 49, 50, 62, 63, 64, 65, 66, 67, 68, 69, 70, 71, 76, 86, 88, 89, 113, 165, 181, 185, 187, 188, 195. Daniel Forster/Talbot Wilson/PPL: 93. Dave Porter/PPL: 116. Dave Smyth/PPL: 33. David Freeman/PPL: 114. Graham Franks/PPL: 115. Icom UK Ltd: 182, 183. Jon Nash/PPL: 116, 127. Lewmar Marine: 66. Matt Evans/PPL: 18, 22, 24, 25, 26, 27, 32, MCA : 190/1. Neil Grundy/PPL: 34, 35, 36. Nick Kirk: pages 6, 19, 44/5, 118, UKSA: 6,7, 30, 96, 115, 134, 142, 152, 166, 184. Northshore Yachts: page 7, 16, 17, 38, 46/7, 66, 67, 111, 163. PPL Photo Agency: 117, 119. Raymarine: 189. Rob Humphreys Yacht Design: pages 48/9. Roy Roberts/PPL: 113. Seldén Masts: 72.